AF687854

The Technical SEO Handbook

By: Roggie Clark

Copyright

Title: The Technical SEO Handbook
Author: Roggie Clark

Cover Design: Roggie Clark
Editing: Renee' Clark

Printed in the United States of America

Disclaimer

The views and opinions expressed in this book are those of the author and do not necessarily reflect the official policy or position of any individual, company, or organization cited or referenced in the text.

The author is not affiliated with any of the individuals, companies, or organizations mentioned in the text, nor does the author receive any form of compensation for citing or referencing them. Some sample scenarios in this text are fictitious. Any similarity to actual persons, living or dead, is coincidental.

The professional information (strategies, tips, and concepts) in this text is distributed on an "as is" basis, without warranty. While every precaution has been taken in the preparation of the text to ensure all information is accurate, neither the author nor the publisher shall have any liability to any person or entity with respect to any loss or damage caused or alleged to be caused directly or indirectly by the instructions contained in this text or by the computer software and hardware products described in it.

Neither the author nor the publisher guarantees any specific results or outcomes, and the information provided in this text should not be construed as professional advice. Readers should always consult with a qualified professional before making any significant changes to their website or business.

By reading this text, you agree that the author nor the publisher is responsible for any direct, indirect, incidental, or consequential damages that may arise from the use of the information provided. You assume full responsibility for any actions taken based on the information presented in this text.

Table of Contents

Chapter 1: Introduction

Welcome to the exciting world of Technical SEO, where the intricacies of the digital realm converge with the art and science of search engine optimization. If you're holding this book in your hands, or perhaps scrolling through its digital pages, you're already on the path to unlocking the secrets of this critical aspect of SEO.

In this ever-evolving digital landscape, where the algorithms of search engines undergo constant refinement, the significance of technical SEO cannot be overstated. It's the engine that powers your website's visibility in the vast sea of online content.

As an author, practitioner, and enthusiast of this field, I have poured my heart and soul into creating a resource that will empower you to navigate the complexities of technical SEO with confidence.

Throughout these pages, you'll find a treasure trove of knowledge, strategies, and techniques that I've meticulously curated to help you elevate your technical SEO skills. Whether you're a seasoned SEO professional looking to refine your expertise or a newcomer eager to grasp the fundamentals, this book is designed to cater to your needs.

From the fundamentals of crawling and indexing to advanced topics like structured data and website speed optimization, I've left no stone unturned in providing you with a comprehensive and accessible resource.

So, whether you're reading this book in the quiet solitude of your study or the bustling atmosphere of a coffee shop, I encourage you to embrace this journey with an open mind and an eagerness to learn.

By the time you reach the final page, you'll have gained the knowledge and skills necessary to improve your website's technical SEO and, in turn, make a significant impact on your online presence.

Thank you for choosing this book, and I'm excited to be your guide on this exciting adventure into the realm of Technical SEO. Let's begin!

What is Technical SEO

Considered to be the foundation of a strong SEO campaign, **Technical SEO** is the domain of SEO that is focused on creating and optimizing a website so that Search engines can readily crawl, render, index, and serve its content (Indig, 2022). These modifications allow search engines to efficiently:

- Crawl: Find essential web pages, and visit them

- Render: Examine the webpages and determine what they are about
- Index: Store the web pages for future use
- Serve search results: Show the webpage to users

It is critical to understand and optimize each step of the search engine's process in order to create a successful and profitable SEO campaign for your website.

Why Does Technical SEO Matter

Technical SEO is critical because Search engines generally “budget” or cap the amount of time they allot to each website for crawling and indexing. (Google Search Central, n.d.).

So if a website is difficult to crawl, there is very little chance of having SEO success, as the website’s content would never reach the index in the first place, and thus would never be seen by searchers.

Additionally, having a slow website speed can lead to users abandoning your website prematurely or not taking the desired actions when they are there.

Having a technically sound website is not just for improving rankings, it is also about improving your conversion funnel to help visitors eventually convert into customers.

Technical SEO Vs. On-Page Vs. Link-Building

Technical SEO is different from the other two domains of SEO. While On-Page SEO focuses on optimizing your website's user-facing elements, technical SEO is about fixing backend components.

Technical SEO is also different from Link-Building which is about building brand awareness and online authority.

Last Words

Now that you understand what technical SEO is and why it matters, let's explore each of the components of Technical SEO that are worth optimizing for a beginner.

Chapter 2: Technical SEO Components

In this book, we are going to explore several key technical components that can be improved or included on a website. As you dive deeper into learning technical SEO on your own, you will find other components that are worth optimizing, but for right now understanding these core components is the most relevant to a beginner. So here they are:

- Web Hosting
- URLs
- Server Response Codes
- Robots.txt File
- XML Sitemap File
- No Index Meta Tag
- Canonical Tag
- Hreflang Tag
- Core Web Vitals
- Schema Markup

By attending to these technical components, you can ensure that crawlers are able to make the best use of their limited crawling resources, and thus increase your chances of achieving maximum SEO success.

Let's go over these components in detail.

Web Hosting

Before I dive into the elements of technical SEO that can be improved, I think that it is important to also mention one factor that is often out of a webmaster's control, and that is **Web Hosting**.

In order for a website to be accessible on the internet, and thus accessible to search engines, the website must be "housed" or stored on a **Server**. A server can also be thought of as a digital neighborhood.

Many webmasters may choose to house their website on their own server, but generally, this is outsourced to a "web hosting service" or companies that have a network or collection of servers that they then "rent" out for other people to house their website (Wikipedia n.d).

While this may seem like a good idea in theory, using shared hosting can lead to an overall slow website performance, and delayed usability of the website.

This can happen due to a variety of factors such as; competition with other websites for server space, the size of the server, how fast the server can process requests, the amount of data that can be transferred at one time, and the amount of traffic the website receives (Donahole, 2020).

In my experience, often the only way to truly mitigate hosting issues is to upgrade (pay for) a better package or to have a dedicated server, which again requires an investment. With both methods being rather expensive for a small business, it is not always feasible to drastically improve performance.

Again, I think that is important for you to know this before you partake in learning the rest of the technical SEO elements because I for one have made the mistake of optimizing a website, without realizing that there were limitations to how far I could go.

Last Words About Web Hosting

Generally, you should choose Web hosting that fits your needs, but sometimes the hosting that is required is outside of the budget you have set aside for it.

I think it is important to understand the role that hosting plays in the overall Technical SEO strategy because it will help you better prioritize actions that actually move the needle, and lead to better performance. Rather than spinning your wheels trying to fix something that may be outside the scope of your immediate needs or control.

Okay now that we discussed Web hosting, let's now talk about the next most important thing, and that is the location on the internet that a website and its page is stored, called a URL.

URLs

A **Uniform Resource Locator (URL)**, also referred to as a "web address", is the location of a website or file on the internet. It was developed in 1994 by Tim Berners-Lee as a way to make the World Wide Web easier to use and more accessible (Wikipedia, 2022).

As I mentioned in the *History Of Search Engines* section of the book, sharing files in the 1*990s* was a cumbersome process, but by making the address of a file easy to remember, Berners-Lee made the process of sharing webpages much easier. Here's an example of a basic URL:

https://www.domain.com/folder/web-page

Let's break down the structure of the URL above. I do want to preface that URLs can be rather tricky to comprehend because they can include a number of components that can be a bit abstract.

But don't worry, in the next section, you can refer to this simple diagram below to get a clear understanding of what I mean:

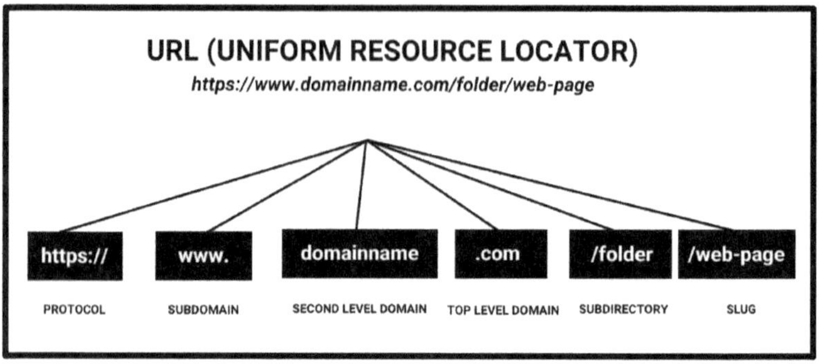

The first piece of a URL is: `https: //` this stands for the *Protocol* or the way the website is accessed.

In this case, it is the **HyperText Transfer Protocol Secure (HTTPS)** which is considered to be the most secure way of transferring information on the internet, as opposed to `http: //` which is just **HyperText Transfer Protocol (HTTP)**, which is often avoided because of its less secure nature. (Moz n.d.).

Next, `www` stands for the World Wide Web. This statement is used to be able to access other webpages in the online directory (Wikipedia, 2022).

`www` is also an example of a **Subdomain.** Which can be thought of as a "subdivision" of a *domain* where additional webpages and content can be stored.

`domainname` is the name of the website (Moz n.d.). It can also be referred to as the **Second level domain (SLD)** or just simply the *domain.*

The `.com` indicates the type of **Top Level Domain (TLD)**, used in the **Domain Naming System (DNS)**. In this case, it is **commercial** (.com), but other common TLDs are `.edu` for education or `.org` for organizations (Moz n.d.).

`/folder` indicates the current **Subdirectory** or holding place of the webpage, and lastly, `/web-page/` is the name of the webpage, it can also be referred to as a **Slug.**

Why Does URL Structure Matter In SEO

Google mentions that having URLs that include "simple" and "descriptive" words can make it easier for users to understand the focus of the webpage (Google Search Central n.d.).

But many SEO practitioners also believe that there is a "ranking" benefit from including descriptive terms in a URL.

According to Moz (n.d.):

> URLs are a minor ranking factor search engines use when determining a particular page or resource's relevance to a search query. While they do give weight to the authority of the overall domain itself, keyword use in a URL can also act as a ranking factor.
>
> While using a URL that includes keywords can improve your site's search visibility, URLs themselves generally do not have a major impact on a page's ability to rank. (paras. 10 -11)

Essentially, Moz is saying by including keywords in a URL, there may be some type of benefit, but again there is no definitive proof from Google's documentation that it does.

Last Words About URL Structure

URLs are the main access point a user has to a website and/or webpage, and many search engines like Google recommend using URLs that are descriptive and intelligible for humans. But, additionally SEO professionals believe that there is a ranking benefit from attending to this measure.

While I haven't found anything in any of the major search engine documentations (Google, Bing and Yahoo!) that vouches for this claim made by many SEOs, I do think it is still worth attending to if you wish to make your URLs easier to read for website visitors in general.

In the next section, we are going to explore some **Response Codes** or alerts that a server gives when a URL request is made, or if there is an error that occurred during the request.

Server Response Codes

When using a server, there are a multitude of problems that may arise from time to time that can affect the performance and SEO score of a website. Some common server response codes you will deal with in SEO are:

- **200** (OK)
- **500** (Internal Server Error)
- **503** (Service Unavailable)
- **404** (Not Found)
- **301** (Moved Permanently)
- **307** (Temporary Redirect)

A `200` response means that the server is able to find the URL and send it to the users. Basically, everything is working fine.

`500` and `503` are generally out of your control, as this indicates that the *"server is unavailable"* (Avira, n.d.). In my experience, this happens when the web hosting company is having technical issues.

404 Not Found

In terms of `404` (Not found), these errors are typically within your control. This type of error indicates that a URL link is either *broken*, the content doesn't exist or the server cannot return the content that is found at the URL. As you can see from the image below, an error page with a specific message is often displayed when this happens:

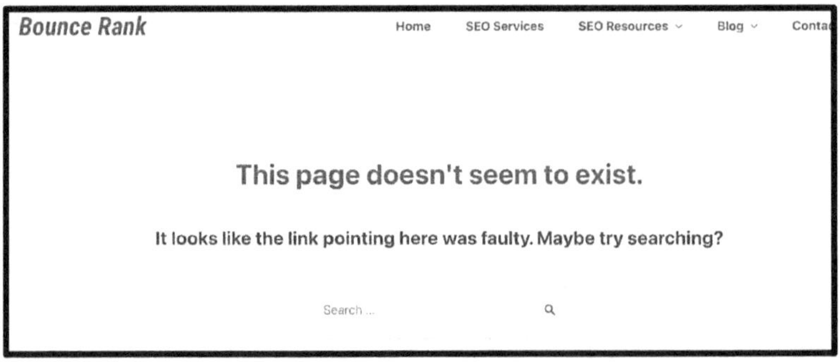

From my experience, 404s can arise for one of three reasons:

1. The URL of the link was not entered correctly
2. The webpage was "unpublished" or may not exist yet
3. The webpage was deleted

If it is reason 1, then it is just as simple as entering the correct URL, problem is resolved.

If it is reason 2, then it is just as simple as publishing the page on the website or creating one.

For reason 3, you need to redirect the old URL to a new URL; and to do this you would implement a **301 (redirect)**.

301 Redirects

The name `301` comes from the response that the server gives when a user accesses the URL but the web content has been "moved permanently" (Payne, 2021).

Essentially, this occurs when the webmaster implements a redirect to a new URL, this is often done via a "plugin" or tool.

Below, I have an image of what the plugin may look like, as you can see, you enter in the old URL or the *Source URL*, then put in the new one, as the *Target URL* and then lastly, press *save* to have it redirected.

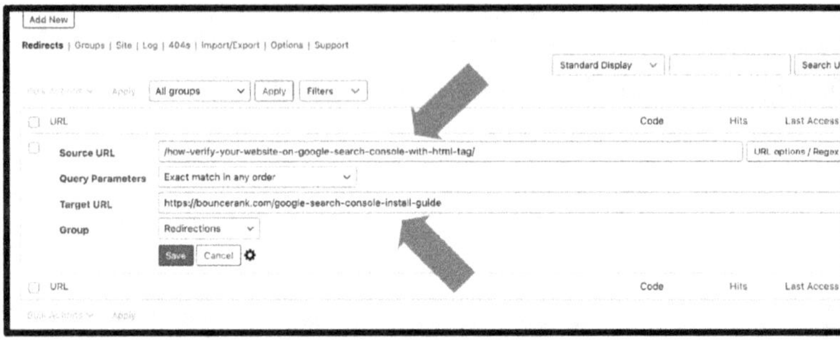

In addition to 301 redirects, there are also **307 redirects** which are used for temporary redirects. These are usually recommended by SEOs to be avoided for security reasons, but it is still an option available to webmasters.

Last Words About Server Response Codes

In my opinion it is important to understand Server response codes so you can quickly diagnose technical problems that may arise, and be able to fix them.

But also it is important to understand the meaning of these codes, especially 500, 503, and 404s because having blocked or broken pages can lead to a poor user experience. Which over time may result in poor search engine rankings.

In the next section, we are going to explore two files that are generally stored on a website that can help search crawlers with crawling and indexing a website. The **Robots.txt File** and the **XML Sitemap**.

Robots.txt File

Pioneered by Martijn Kojer in 1994, the *Robots Exclusion Protocol,* now simply known as the **Robots.txt file**, is a file generally stored on a website at the URL slug; `/robots.txt`

It was invented as a way to tell search engine web crawlers which directories or web folders on the website the crawler can access. The file can also be used to specify which folders the crawlers are "blocked" or *should not/ cannot* access on a website (Wall, 2017).

In a nutshell, the robots.txt file contains "directives" "rules" and "references" or which can be thought of as a request to search crawlers regarding the directories you wish to be visited or ignored.

However, I must emphasize, it is only a request, and there is no guarantee the search crawler will "obey" it.

Here is what Google Search Central (2022) has to say on the matter:

> The instructions in robots.txt files cannot enforce crawler behavior to your site; it's up to the crawler to obey them. While Googlebot and other

respectable web crawlers obey the instructions in a robots.txt file, other crawlers might not (para. 8).

Based on the quote above from Google, generally speaking, crawlers will follow the request most of the time, but I want to pose a caveat because the way they process the request and utilize them when choosing how and what content to index, does vary.

It is much easier to explain this in context, so let me first introduce to you, a basic robots.txt file. Here's how a basic file is formatted:

```
User-agent: *
Disallow: /author/
Allow: /author/archives/

Sitemap: https://bouncerank.com/sitemap_index.xml
```

The file is broken up into three main components:

- User-Agent
- Disallow/Allow Rule
- Sitemap Reference

User-Agent Directive

The **User-Agent** directive specifies what Search crawlers are able to visit a website. A "star" or * next to the user-agent indicates that all search crawlers are allowed to visit the website. Here's what they may look like

```
User-agent: *
```

But if you want to specify a specific search crawler, then you would add another user-agent directive and include the *code* of the crawler you wish to add. Here are some common crawler codes (Eaton, 2022):

```
Googlebot - Google
```

```
Bingbot - Bing
```

```
Slurp - Yahoo!
```

```
DuckDuckBot - DuckDuckGo
```

To include a specific crawler in the file, it may look like this:

```
User-agent: Bingbot
```

Generally speaking, specific crawlers are only specified if the webmaster wishes to limit access to a website for a particular crawler.

In order to explain how to block a specific crawler, I must first explain the **Disallow** and **Allow** rules, and how they are used in conjunction with the user-agent directive to block a specific web crawler.

Disallow And Allow Rules

The **Disallow Rule** tells crawlers which web folder/ subdirectories it should not visit or are "blocked from". It can also be used to specify which crawlers should not visit the website at all, as I mentioned earlier.

Also, you may sometimes see an **Allow Rule**; this is the opposite of a *disallow rule*, as it tells the search crawlers what subdirectory they can visit that is *inside* of another subdirectory (Content King, 2022).

Essentially with the *allow rule*, a webmaster can allow crawlers to visit a specific secondary directory, even though the top-level directory may be blocked by the *disallow rule.* To recall the screenshot again:

```
User-agent: *
Disallow: /author/
Allow: /author/archives/

Sitemap: https://bouncerank.com/sitemap_index.xml
```

As you can see, I specified in the `Disallow:` rule that I want to block crawlers from visiting the `/author/` top level directory on my website, but with the `Allow:` rule I specified that crawlers are able to visit the

`/archives/` second level directory, that is inside the `/author/` directory.

It is not uncommon to see a robots.txt file that contains a *disallow rule*, but not an allow rule and the reason is generally speaking, the *allow rule* is *implied.* What I mean by that is, if a `disallow:` rule is specified, without an `allow:` rule, it is essentially being communicated to the web crawler that the whole directory is blocked from crawling.

So unless the webmaster wants to specify a specific directory in the blocked directory to be crawled, then the rule is often left out.

As you can see in the screenshot below, I included only a *disallow rule*, and I specified that I want the `/author/`directory blocked from crawling.

```
User-agent: *
Disallow: /author/

Sitemap: https://bouncerank.com/sitemap_index.xml
```

Additionally, with the rules, you are able to specify multiple directories that you want to block or allow to be crawled. For instance, If I want to *disallow* multiple folders, I would simply add another *disallow rule:*

```
Disallow: /admin/
Disallow: /about/
```

As you can see in the code snippet example, I wanted to also block my `/admin/` and `/about/` directories. Again the same thing can be done for the *allow rule*, if I wanted to allow a *lower-level directory* to be crawled in each of these directories, my file would look like this:

```
Allow: /admin/plugins/
Allow: /about/bio-pages/
Disallow: /admin/
Disallow: /about/
```

One last thing that I want to point out, it is very important to include the "slashes" or `//` between the directories names that you are blocking or allowing to be crawled.

```
/directory-name/
```

Reason being is the symbols make it clear to crawlers that a "folder" or directory is being specified in the rule. Essentially; without the slashes, the rule would be invalid. Now let's discuss how to block search crawlers.

Blocking Search Crawlers

As I mentioned earlier, in addition to blocking a specific directory, a specific crawler can be blocked from crawling entirely. In order to do this, a webmaster can include a `User-agent:` directive with the crawler code they wish to block, and then include a `Disallow:` rule with a slash `/`

The slash `/` indicates that the search crawler is barred from visiting all directories; essentially the whole website. It looks like this:

```
User-agent: Bingbot
Disallow: /
```

Additionally, all crawlers can be blocked, by including a `User-agent:` directive with a star `*` and a `disallow:` rule with a slash `/`

```
User-Agent: *
Disallow: /
```

Generally speaking, you want to avoid having this configuration in your robots.txt file, but there may be times where you wish to block crawlers entirely. For instance, if you are performing a website migration and you do not want crawlers visiting the new website until it's done, then that may be a good time to include this specific configuration in the file.

Now let's get into the last component of the file, which is the *Sitemap Reference.*

Sitemap Reference

The **Sitemap Reference** tells crawlers the URL, or page path, to get to the sitemap. In the next section, I will explain in detail what a *Sitemap* is and why a website may benefit from one, but for now, just know that it is essentially a "map" search crawlers use to find webpages on a website.

As you can see in the screenshot, to include the sitemap reference you can just write the URL of the sitemap:

```
User-agent: *
Disallow: /author/
Allow: /author/archives/

Sitemap: https://bouncerank.com/sitemap_index.xml
```

For my website Bounce Rank, the rule would look like this:

```
Sitemap: https://bouncerank.com/
sitemap_index.xml
```

And that is the last component you need to include in the file.

Last Words About Robots.txt File

Despite the intricacies of the Robots.txt file, it is honestly not required to include on a website, but it is generally best practice to include one.

The reason is, that the file gives webmasters the opportunity to tell search engines what folders they should crawl, and which ones they do not.

By being able to control what is indexed and crawled, you can help search crawlers better prioritize indexing content that matters to users, and avoid wasting crawl resources on content that is not relevant.

Now let’s discuss the next technical SEO component: The **XML Sitemap**.

XML Sitemap

Another file stored on a website that tells search engine crawlers about the organization of a website’s pages is known as the **XML Sitemap**. It is generally stored on a website at the URL slug; `/sitemap.xml`

The file essentially is a “map” that shows Web crawlers how to access each *URL* or location of content on the domain; hence the name “sitemap”.

Additionally, the file indicates to search crawlers the priority/ hierarchy of pages on the website, and lastly, it can be used to alert search engines about changes to the website.

XML refers to the coding language, *Extensive Markup Language* used to create the file. To give you a bit more context:

The use of XML for sitemaps dates back to 2005 when Google launched *The sitemap 0.84 protocol.* As websites were becoming more and more complex, search engines found it increasingly more difficult to track the numerous changes that website owners were making to their sites. (DynoMapper n.d.)

"This led to the creation of XML protocol that made it possible for search engines to effectively track the URLs and boost their search through the placement of all the information in a single page" (DynoMapper n.d.).

Essentially by using XML, search engines are now able to access webpages easier. Here's an example of a basic XML sitemap configuration:

```
<?xml version="1.0" encoding="UTF-8"?>
<urlset xmlns="http://www.sitemaps.org/schemas/sitemap/0.9">
<url>
      <loc>https://bouncerank.com/author/rajseo333/</loc>
   </url>
   <url>
      <loc>https://bouncerank.com/what-is-seo/</loc>
   </url>
   <url>
      <loc>https://bouncerank.com/how-to-write-seo-specialist-cover-letter/</loc>
   </url>
   </urlset>
```

To help explain in detail the parts of the sitemap, I want to recall Yoast's article *What is an XML sitemap and why should you have one?* and Woorank's article *What is an XML sitemap?* A sitemap includes the following information per Yoast's (2022) and Woorank's (n.d.) articles:

Sitemap Structure

The first piece is the XML version declaration, which tells search engine crawlers what type of file they are reading:

```
<?xml version="1.0" encoding="UTF-8'?>
```

The next part is the <urlset> HTML tag which tells search engines about the protocol.

```
<urlset xmlns="http://www.sitemaps.org/schemas/sitemap/0.9"/
>
```

The third part of the sitemap includes the `<url>` HTML tag and the `<loc>` tag *nested* within it. The `<loc>` tag is used to designate the absolute URL, or location on the website of the webpage.

```
<url>
    <loc>https://bouncerank.com/
author/rajseo333</loc>
</url>
```

`<url>` tag and the `<loc>` tag configuration can be duplicated to include additional URLs that are located on the website. Again to recall the screenshot, as you can see, the URLs:

- https://bouncerank.com/what-is-seo/
- https://bouncerank.com/how-to-write-seo-specialist-cover-letter/

Were also included in the sitemap each placed in a `<loc>` tag ***nested*** in `<url>` tag.

```
<?xml version="1.0" encoding="UTF-8"?>
<urlset xmlns="http://www.sitemaps.org/schemas/sitemap/0.9">
<url>
      <loc>https://bouncerank.com/author/rajseo333/</loc>
   </url>
   <url>
      <loc>https://bouncerank.com/what-is-seo/</loc>
   </url>
   <url>
      <loc>https://bouncerank.com/how-to-write-seo-specialist-cover-letter/</loc>
   </url>
   </urlset>
```

Lastly, while it is not included in the screenshot, there is an additional tag that can be included in the sitemap `<lastmod>` tag which indicates the last time the sitemap was updated.

```
<lastmod>2022-01-01</lastmod>
```

As I mentioned earlier, this is how a basic XML sitemap is constructed, but the elements/tags that are included can vary depending on the desired outcome and usage by the webmaster.

Last Words About XML Sitemaps

Similar to Robots.txt Files, XML Sitemaps are not required by search engines and do not speed up crawling and/or indexing. But again, it is generally good SEO hygiene to include one on a website.

Also, as I mentioned earlier in the *Robots.txt* section, you want to ensure that you include a sitemap reference in your Robots.txt file. Again this can help make it easier for crawlers to find your sitemap and thus make the best use of it.

In the next section, we are going to come back to another term that I mentioned earlier in this book, and that is a **No Index Meta tag**. We are going to talk about what they are and how they can be helpful to use.

Noindex Meta Tag

The `noindex` rule, also sometimes referred to as a **Noindex Meta Tag** or just simply the *No index tag*, is a directive that can be specified in the **Robots Meta tag,** a tag placed in the HTML `<head>` of a webpage.

The rule is used to tell search engines not to index or include a specific URL/webpage in their database (Ahrefs n.d.).

Below is an example of what the code snippet may look like:

```
<meta name="robots" content="noindex">
```

The no index tag is considered to be a *directive* or an almost exact order that search engines follow. The reason I say almost "exact" because *most* search engines will follow the directive, Google for one does:

"When Googlebot crawls that page and extracts the tag or header, Google will drop that page entirely from Google Search results, regardless of whether other sites link to it". (Google Search Central, 2023)

Many SEO professionals such as myself, generally recommend using the no index tag instead of *disallowing* a webpage in the Robots.txt file for content that you do not want to be indexed by search engines.

The reason being is, that content that is blocked can still be crawled by the search engines and indexed. This can be an issue, as crawling resources would be wasted on a page that is blocked. So keep that in mind when implementing no index tags.

Last Words About The Noindex Meta Tag

The No index meta tag is rather straightforward, essentially you want to use it to control what content you want or do not want search engines to index.

The disallow directive in the Robots.txt File also can be used to "block" search engines from certain URLs; however, search engines can ignore this directive, and crawl and potentially index your page.

The no index meta tag is the most effective way to ensure that URLs you do not want indexed will be "hidden" from search engines. In the next section, we are going to explore two more additional tags; ***Canonicals*** and ***Hreflangs***.

Canonical Tag

A **Canonical Tag** `rel="canonical"` is a piece of HTML code that is added to webpages to tell search engines which page is the original or the preferred version of a page to index (Hardwick, 2022).

Generally, the tag is used to mitigate crawling issues that may arise when multiple pages on a website contain the same or similar information, this is often referred to as ***Duplicate content***. (Google Search Central, n.d.)

There are many ways to specify a *canonical*, but the most common is via the HTML `<head>` element of the webpage deemed to be the duplicate.

In the `<head>` section, this HTML code snippet below is added:

```
<link rel="canonical" href="https://
example.com/sample-page"/>
```

The `<link>` element indicates that you are linking to another page; the `rel="canonical"` indicates which page is a duplicate of another page, and then the `href="https://example.com/sample-page/"` indicates the URL of the page you are setting as the original source of content.

Here's a diagram to help you make sense of this concept:

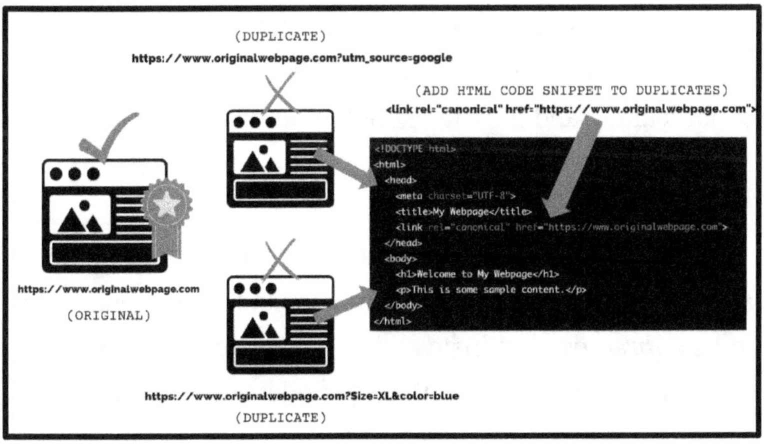

As you can see in the diagram, the preferred version is:

```
https://www.originalwebpage.com
```

To indicate to search engines that this is the original source of content, as you can see in the diagram, you add the code snippet (shown below) to each of the duplicate pages' HTML `<head>` element:

```
<link rel="canonical" href="https://
www.originalwebpage.com"/>
```

Last Words About The Canonical Tag

Generally the Canonical tag is the preferred method to specify to search engines the original source of a piece of content, in instances where there is duplicate content in the index.

While every website owner may not deal with duplicate content, it is important to be aware of the canonical tag and how it can help you with your SEO efforts.

I do want to preface that, while a webmaster can add a canonical tag to a webpage, the tag is not considered to be a *directive*, but instead a *hint* to search engines on which is the canonical or the most relevant page version.

So just because a tag is specified, does not mean that the search engines will obey it, so keep that in mind, if and when you choose to implement the tag. Okay in the next section let's discuss **Hreflang Tags**.

Hreflang Tag

An **Hreflang Tag** is a piece of HTML code that you add to a webpage's `<head>` element to indicate to search engines the languages and countries you are targeting for an alternate version of the webpage.

Essentially, the snippet is used to help search engines show the correct copy of the page to users in a specific language and country. Here's an example of what the code snippet looks like (Google Search central, n.d.):

```
<link rel="alternate"
hreflang="lang_code" href="url_of_page"
/>
```

The `<link>` HTML element indicates that you are linking to another page, the `rel="alternate"` indicates the relationship between the two linked documents and that they are different versions of the same page.

The `hreflang="lang_code"` is where you insert the specific code for the language you wish to target, such as *en* for English, `fr` for French, `es` for Spanish or *de* for German (Pokorny, 2022).

Lastly, the `hreflang="url_of_page"` is the URL of the page you wish to associate with the alternate language. This is the webpage that you want to be shown to users in another language. Here's a diagram to help you make sense of this concept:

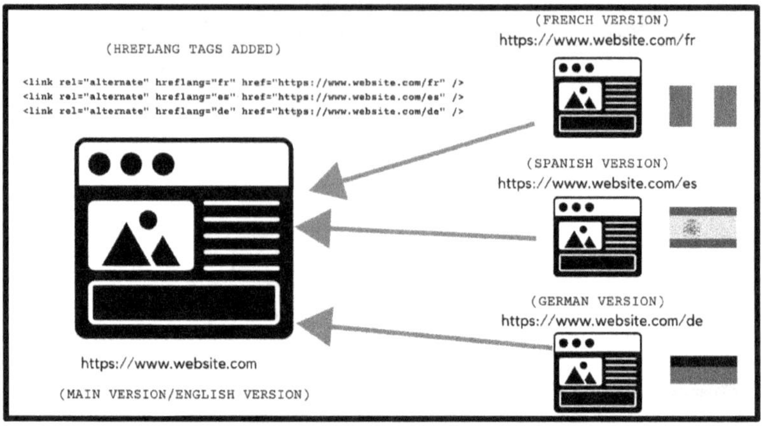

As you can see in the diagram above, the main version or English version of the page: `https://www.website.com` , has three hreflang tags added to it; one for each alternate language version of the website; *French*, *Spanish* and *German*. As you can see in the code snippets below:

```
<link rel="alternate" hreflang="fr"
href="https://www.website.com/fr" />
<link rel="alternate" hreflang="es"
href="https://www.website.com/es" />
<link rel="alternate" hreflang="de"
href="https://www.website.com/de" />
```

The `hreflang` elements of each tag includes the language codes; *`fr`* (french), `es` (Spanish) and *`de`* (German), and then the href attributes include the corresponding copy of the page for that language.

The desired outcome is that search engines will recognize the content as being available in alternate languages, so that when users are in France they will see the French version of the page, if they are in Spain they will see the Spanish, and if they are in Germany they will see the German version of the page.

Why Do Hreflang Tags Matter For SEO

Hreflang tags serve several key purposes for SEO. First, they are used to indicate the relationship between different language versions of a page, helping to keep your website relevant in the eyes of search engines and your visitors, wherever they are in the world.

De Valk (2022) reports:

> If you have a version of a page that you have optimized for the users' language and location, you want them to land on that page. Because having the correct language and location-dependent information improves their user experience and thus leads to fewer people bouncing back to the search

> results. And fewer people bouncing back to the search results leads to higher rankings. (para. 6)

Second, they prevent instances of duplicate content from being shown to the same users in different countries.

De Valk (2022) continues:

> If you have the same content in English on different URLs aimed at the UK, the US, and Australia, the difference on these pages might be as small as a change in prices and currency. But without hreflang, Google might not understand what you're trying to do and see it as duplicate content. With hreflang, you make it very clear to the search engine that it's (almost) the same content, just optimized for different people. (para. 7)

Google also recommends that you use hreflang tags preemptively, rather than have them decide on which copy of the page to use:

“Note that even without taking action, Google might still find alternate language versions of your page, but it is usually best for you to explicitly indicate your language- or region-specific pages” (Google Search central, n.d.).

Again, highlights the benefit of using this tag for SEO.

Last Words About Hreflang Tags

Hreflang tags are primarily used for *International SEO*, but it still may be beneficial to know them and have some understanding of how they work.

Also, based on Google's recommendations, it is important to use them if you wish to have a quality user experience across regions and languages, if you have multiple versions of your site.

In the next section, we are going to explore the **Core Web Vitals**, and how they are used to assess the overall speed and performance of a website.

Core Web Vitals

The **Core Web Vitals** is a report provided by Google that shows the performance of each website's unique webpages or URLs. It essentially assesses a website’s overall user experience (UX), speed, and performance based on actual user data.

The report is grouped by (Google Search Central, 2022):

- Status (Poor, Need improvement, Good)
- Metric type (CLS, INP, LCP)
- URL group (groups of similar webpages)

A report is provided for both the Mobile and Desktop versions of a website.

Stox (2022) reports:

> The data comes from the Chrome User Experience Report (CrUX), which records data from opted-in Chrome users. The metrics are assessed at the 75th percentile of users. So if 70% of your users are in the “good” category and 5% are in the “need improvement” category, then your page will still be judged as “need improvement. (para. 8)

Essentially the report measures the webpages overall *User experience (UX)* and performance. In other words, the report assesses how easy it is for a user and search crawler to navigate and access each component of a webpage.

The colloquial of just saying *"Core Web Vitals"* appears to come from the three metrics that Google measures to compare each URL based on user data (Google Search Central, 2023):

- CLS - Cumulative Layout Shift
- INP - Interactive to Next Paint
- LCP - Largest Contentful Paint

Many SEO professionals believe that improving on these three metrics will lead to more favorable rankings on search engine result pages.

Here are Stox's (2022) thoughts on the matter:

> There are over 200 ranking factors, many of which don't carry much weight. When talking about Core Web Vitals, Google reps have referred to these as tiny ranking factors or even tiebreakers. (para. 14)

As Stox highlights in the statement above, improving core web vitals will not create a significant ranking boost; however, we can *assume* that in the event that two incredibly similar websites are competing for a ranking position - Google will essentially favor the website with better core web vitals.

BacklinkO (n.d.) expands on this topic and reports the following:

> It's important to point out that a great page experience score won't magically push you to the #1 spot in Google. In fact, Google was quick to point out that page experience is one of several (approximately 200) factors that they use to rank sites in search. (para. 8)

While it may not lead to an alarming ranking boost, it may still be worth improving in order to improve the quality of a website as a whole.

Now let's explore each specific core web vital metric outlined in the report, in greater detail.

Largest Contentful Paint

Largest Contentful Paint (LCP) is a measure of how long it takes the "largest content element" to render and become visible in a user's device viewport, from the moment in time when the user first visits the webpage.

Google points out that this is often a *picture, or video* (Google Search Central, n.d.).

It is measured in seconds, with an LCP of *2.5 seconds* or less being the desired score for optimal performance; anything over *4 seconds* being a possible reason for alarm.

The LCP is arguably the most important part of the report, as it is a key factor that Google uses to evaluate a website's speed performance, and because of that, it may be worth improving for a sound SEO strategy.

According to Rocket Content (2020):

> Over the past few years, Google has increasingly focused on defining evaluation parameters to enhance the user experience, all of them integrating Core Web Vitals.
>
> As LCP is related to page loading time, it naturally influences how Google analyzes and ranks a site on the results page". (para. 21)

If you run into problems while optimizing LCP, it may be helpful to visit Web.dev to learn more about how LCP works and how you can improve it.

Interactive to Next Paint

A new metric by Google that is replacing the FID (First Input Delay). While FID measures the time it takes for the webpage to respond to the first click or interaction a user makes, INP measures the time it takes for the webpage to respond to all clicks, taps, and keyboard interactions.

Essentially, it measures the page's overall responsiveness and assesses the page's ability to provide a good user experience throughout the lifespan of the page.

According to Wagner (2023): The goal of INP is to ensure the time from when a user initiates an interaction until the next frame is painted is as short as possible, for all or most interactions the user makes.

An INP below or at 200 milliseconds means your page has good responsiveness. Anything over 500ms is considered failing.

Again similar to FID, a slow INP score can indicate that Javascript events or CSS styles are taking too long to parse. It may also be impacted by an image that is taking too long to load. Similar to Javascript, HTML is parsed line by line, so having a large image or video may impact this score as well.

Cumulative Layout Shift

Cumulative layout shift (CLS) is the sum of all individual layout shift scores for every unexpected movement of the webpage that occurs while it is in use.

This metric is evaluated by numbers between zero and 1, with a CLS of *0.1* being the target, and a CLS of over *0.25* indicating a need for improvement (Google Search Central, n.d.).

Similar to the LCP, an image or video is often the reason for a poor score.

Walton (2019) states:

> The culprit might be an image or video with unknown dimensions, a font that renders larger or smaller than its fallback, or a third-party ad or widget that dynamically resizes itself. (para. 3)

Additionally, Google Search Central (n.d.) reports:

> This is important because having pages elements shift while a user is trying to interact with it is a bad user experience. If you can't seem to find the reason for a high value, try interacting with the page to see how that affects the score (para. 11)

For more information on how to improve CLS scores visit Web.dev's article; *Optimize Cumulative Layout Shift*.

Last Words About Core Web Vitals

I wanted to provide you with information on the Core Web Vitals in an objective fashion to help you better understand them.

My hope is that this information will help you make an informed decision about whether you should improve the core web vitals, or *if you are even able to*.

As I mentioned earlier in the chapter, Web hosting can often be an unexpected, and uncontrollable limitation on your website's ability to achieve optimal speed and performance.

But additionally I've found in my experience also having a thin *Content Management System (CMS)* can poorly impact your core web vitals as well. As they often have built-in limitations that keep you from achieving a pristine score.

So it may be worth it to keep this information in mind as you consider your strategy for improving the scores, to see if it is even worth your time.

I also want to point out two additional metrics worth considering when assessing a website's performance:

- **Time To Interactive (TTI)** which measures how long it takes the webpage to be fully usable after being requested (Chrome developers, 2019).
- **First Contentful Paint (FCP)** which is a measure of when the browser first renders any image, video or text (MDN Contributors, 2022).

TTI and FCP are important as they both provide additional context for how well a webpage is able to be rendered and interacted with.

But in general, if you have a firm understanding of the three Core Web Vitals (LCP, FID, CLS) you are more than versed enough to be able to improve a website's speed and performance.

In the next chapter, we are going to explore the last technical SEO component worth attending to for a beginner, and that is: **Schema Markup**.

Schema Markup

Schema Markup, also known as *Schema.org structured data*, is a library of code that includes *microdata* which are "tags" or identifiers you can add to parts of a website's HTML code, to help search engines better read and interpret the context of your content. The library is made up of different types of "markups" that Google, Bing, Yandex, and Yahoo! provided as a joint collaboration (Moz, n.d.).

Being that search engines are mostly a network of computers they don't necessarily understand the "intent" or goal of a piece of web content. Hence, it can be harder for them to deliver the best results to a user searching for a particular piece of information.

According to Google Search Central's YouTube channel (2022):

> The web is a very loosely structured collection of documents…but we need that data to be more structured to apply visual features… while we have

technology to find that "structure" in webpage text automatically, those systems are not perfect, that's where you come in. (Google Search Central, 2022)

Schema markup can help search engines understand the intent of your content by highlighting the most important aspects of your webpage, and letting them know what type of information it contains. For instance, let's imagine your content includes a "question", the search engine may not necessarily understand that it is a *question*, as the goal of your sentence was to gain information about a topic. They may just interpret it as a *statement*.

For instance:

Is pizza made in America? (Question)

May be interpreted as:

Is pizza made in America. (Statement)

But here's where schema markup can help. As you can see in the image below, in the markup, you can format your question in a way that the search engine knows it is a question. This is an example of *FAQ Schema Markup.* As you can see you can also add an "answer" to your question to make it even clearer that this is a question.

```
<script type="application/ld+json">
{
  "@context": "https://schema.org",
  "@type": "FAQPage",
  "mainEntity": {
    "@type": "Question",
    "name": "Is Pizza made in America?",
    "acceptedAnswer": {
      "@type": "Answer",
      "text": "Pizza, as we know it today, has its roots in Italy. However, it was brought to the United States by
Italian immigrants in the late 19th and early 20th centuries. Since then, pizza has become a staple of
American cuisine and has evolved to include many different regional styles and toppings. In the United
States, there are many popular pizza chains and independent pizzerias that make their own unique versions
of pizza. Some of the most well-known American pizza styles include New York-style, Chicago-style, and
California-style pizza.So while pizza itself may have originated in Italy, it has certainly been adapted and
popularized in the United States and is now considered a quintessential American food."
```

Additionally, using schema markup gives you a chance to get an "enhancement", or a *rich snippet.* This is where the webpage search result is larger and takes up more space on the user's screen.

The reason why FAQ markup, and schema markup as a whole, is so prized by SEO professionals is that it is believed that it can increase the likelihood of a user clicking on the result by 30% (Bruemmer, 2011).

While schema markup can lead to correlational SEO improvements, Google clearly highlights that it is not causational, as Schema Markup is not a ranking factor.

According to Google Search Central (2019):

> Where from our point of view, they might have spent more time doing these things technically correct but does that mean the page is actually a

> better search result, is that really something that provides more value to the user or is it just that someone was a little bit smarter in creating that page and the actual content people would read is not actually that much better.
>
> So that's… the tricky balance there and I don't see that changing in the sense that we would suddenly say any page with structured data will have a ranking boost because structured data is invisible so even that would be something that we would be ranking things higher for technical reasons that users would not even be able to appreciate. (Google Search Central, 2019)

But despite this, schema markup's benefits should not be underestimated because even though having it does not lead to an explicit ranking boost, there is clear data that shows searchers do interact more with search results when they see it.

Here are some other types of schema markup that can be added to a website courtesy of (Xu, 2018), I included the list in a table format to help you better understand each of the schema types possible usage for designated parts or types of web content:

Organizational Schema	Generally for companies, or established brands
Person Schema	Generally to highlight a spec important figure or person
Local Business Schema	Generally for businesses that physical locations locally
Product Schema	Generally for eCommerce websites
Breadcrumbs	Used to help users know wha webpage they are on

Article Schema	Generally meant for highligh news articles or editorials
How-To Schema	Generally for highlighting ho guides or step-by-step instru
Video Schema	Generally to highlight video content on a webpage
Recipe Schema	For highlighting recipe conte how-to guides for foods
Event Schema	For highlighting events, shov festivals or concerts

This list is not exhaustive. You can visit Schema.org for a complete list of schema markup types.

Last Words About Schema Markup

Despite not being a ranking factor, Schema Markup is still a great tool to have in your arsenal to increase the potential of someone clicking on your website when they see it on Search engines.

When getting started with schema markup, I would recommend trying out one markup type at a time to see how it affects your website. Not to mention, in my experience when you mix too many schema markup types at once, you run the risk of search engines ignoring the markup completely.

So keep that in mind when testing out different schema markup types.

Last Words

Having a strong understanding of each technical SEO concept is crucial to becoming a successful SEO professional.

Also, in order to properly execute your SEO strategy and rank your website on search engines, you must have an understanding of how to properly execute technical SEO.

In the next chapter, we are going to discuss how to audit for technical SEO issues, so you can see if your website is in a healthy technically.

Chapter 3: Technical Auditing Process

The problem with technical SEO is that it can quickly become confusing and cumbersome to keep up with all the maintenance required.

This can become a big deal if you have a lot of people who use the backend of your website. There's a high chance that something technical may get broken and you are not able to diagnose it and fix it quickly.

This is where a technical SEO checklist can be helpful because it gives you something to quickly follow in order to get things back up and running.

With that being said, here is my technical SEO checklist that you can follow.

Common Technical SEO Tools

In order to do technical SEO properly it may be helpful to have access to a few different tools that can help you find issues and fix them quickly. Below I have listed a few of the most common tools you can use.

1. **Google Search Console**: This is a free tool provided by Google that allows you to monitor your website's performance in Google's search results. It provides valuable data on crawl errors, indexation, and search queries.

2. **Google PageSpeed Insights**: This tool assesses the speed and performance of your web pages on both desktop and mobile devices, providing suggestions for improvement.

3. **Google Lighthouse**: Lighthouse is a browser extension and auditing tool that provides insights into your website's performance, accessibility, best practices, and SEO. It's commonly used for measuring web page quality.

4. **Crawler/Spider Tool**: This is an application that crawls your website to analyze on-page elements such as titles, meta descriptions, header tags, and more. It's useful for identifying technical issues on a website. There are multiple examples of tools, do you research to find the best fit for your needs

Step 1: Check For Multiple Versions of Your Website

Having multiple versions of your website is normal. However, you want to make sure each "version" goes to the same site. For example, `https://www.bouncerank.com` and `http://www.bouncerank.com` are two different versions of our site bouncerank but they should all go to the same site.

How to check the multiple versions of your site:

1. Go to your preferred web browser
2. Type in these 4 different versions of the homepage URL:
    - `http://example.com`
    - `https://example.com`
    - `http://www.example.com`
    - `https://www.example.com`

They should all redirect to one URL. If not, set up 301 redirects to avoid duplicate content problems.

Step 2: Check Indexing

Review the indexed pages of your website in search engines like Google. Compare the number of indexed pages to the actual number of pages on your site to ensure there are no discrepancies.

Here's how to see if you are having indexing issues:

1. Log into your Google Search Console account.
2. Select the "Index coverage" report in Google Search Console and review the result.

You can also follow up by running a crawl on a website crawling software, this will provide you with additional insights on specific pages and issues to fix.

Step 3: Evaluate Website Speed

Check your website's loading speed using tools like Google PageSpeed Insights. This tools will provide insights on areas to optimize, such as image compression, caching, minifying CSS and JavaScript, and reducing server response time.

To check your website's loading speed, do the following:

1. Go to your preferred browser and visit https://pagespeed.web.dev.
2. On the page speed insights website, enter your homepage URL and other important web pages on your site.
3. View the results and see where you need to make improvements.

You want to make a habit of checking your website speed regularly, especially if you website is very picture-heavy, images naturally take up a lot of space and can slow down your website. So keep that in mind as you are optimizing your website for speed.

Step 4: Assess Mobile-Friendliness

Ensure your website is mobile-friendly by using Google's Mobile-Friendly Test or similar tools. Mobile responsiveness is crucial, as search engines prioritize mobile-friendly websites in their rankings. Optimize your website's design and layout to ensure a seamless experience across different devices.

To check your website's mobile friendliness do the following:

1. Using your preferred web browser visit: https://search.google.com/test/mobile-friendly.
2. Enter your website into the test bar.
3. Wait for your results (it may take a minute or two).
4. Review the results (take a screenshot so you can refer back to it later and measure your website's progress over time).

Since 2015, having a mobile-friendly website has been a key factor that search engines use to rank websites. So it is worth your time to invest in a website that is mobile-friendly.

Step 5: Review URL Structure

URLs that are descriptive, have relevant keywords in them, are short and readable, and are preferred by search engines. Also, they are much easier to remember and read for humans.

Here's how to review yours:

1. Gather a list of all your website's URLs.

2. Examine them, Are they descriptive and user-friendly? Do they contain relevant keywords?
3. Make note of this, and for new URLs make sure they are easy to read.

We recommend to clients to not change URLs unless it makes sense to do so. As in the page is not performing well. The reason is, that you will run into major indexing issues. So generally speaking, keep your URLs the same.

Step 6: Check the Robots.txt File

A Robots.txt file is a text file that contains directives for web crawlers (such as Google) that tell them which pages they can and cannot crawl and index. As I mentioned earlier, it is typically found at `/robots.txt`

Here's how to check your robots.txt:

1. Go to the browser and type your domain name in the address bar. At the end of your domain name, include this slug: `/robots.txt`.
2. Type enter, and then view your robots.txt file to ensure it aligns with your website's requirements and goals.
3. Look for User-Agent directives, Review the Allow and Disallow directives to ensure they accurately reflect the areas of your website that should be allowed or disallowed for crawling. If you have

specified the location of your XML sitemap in your robots.txt file, ensure that the sitemap URL is accurate.

4. Validate the Robots.txt File, you can use online tools or validators specifically designed for this purpose. Sign in to the webmaster tools provided by search engines like Google, Bing, or Yandex. Locate the section where you can test or fetch your robots.txt file. Use this feature to ensure that search engines can access and interpret your robots.txt file correctly.

Regularly monitor your website's behavior and search engine crawling patterns to ensure your robots.txt file is functioning as intended. Make updates to the file when necessary, such as when you want to allow or disallow access to specific pages or directories.

Step 7: Check XML Sitemap

An XML sitemap is a file that lists all the URLs on your website and how to find them.

Your XML sitemap is typically located in the root directory of your website. It is often named "`sitemap.xml`" or similar. If you're not sure where to find it, you can check your website's robots.txt file, which usually contains a reference to the sitemap's location.

To check your XML sitemap, follow these steps:

1. Go to the browser and type your domain name in the address bar. At the end of your domain name, including this slug: `/sitemap.xml`
2. Type enter, and then view your sitemap file, Check the structure of your XML sitemap to ensure it follows the proper format. The sitemap should be well-formed XML and include necessary elements like `<urlset>`, `<url>`, `<loc>`, and `<lastmod>`. Each URL entry should have its corresponding `<loc>` element, indicating the URL of the page.
3. Review the list of URLs in your XML sitemap. Make sure that all important pages of your website are included. Check for any missing or omitted pages that should be present in the sitemap. If any URLs are missing, you may need to update your sitemap generation process.
4. Check that your XML sitemap is error-free, you can use online XML sitemap validators. Several free tools are available that allow you to submit your XML sitemap for validation.
5. Once you have confirmed that your XML sitemap is accurate and error-free, submit it to search engines.
6. Sign in to the webmaster tools provided by search engines like Google, Bing, or Yandex, and locate the section where you can submit or add your sitemap. Follow the instructions provided by the specific search engine to submit your XML sitemap.

Regularly monitor your XML sitemap to ensure it stays up to date. Whenever you add or remove pages from your website, make sure to update your XML sitemap accordingly. Additionally, periodically check your search engine's webmaster tools for any reported issues or errors related to your XML sitemap.

Step 8: Verify HTTPS and SSL Certificates

Check if your website is secured with HTTPS and has a valid SSL certificate. HTTPS is an important ranking factor, and it ensures secure communication between your website and users. Make sure all internal and external links are using the HTTPS protocol.

Here's how to do it:

1. Type your website in your browser's address bar, and press enter.
2. Check to see if a "green lock" is displayed on the left side of your browser.
3. Spot-check a few other pages on your website to see if the lock is displayed.
4. If it is not, you need to contact your hosting provider to get an SSL certificate installed.

Having a secure website is not just about ranking, it is also important to have if you plan on keeping sensitive or personal information about your users on your website.

Step 9: Audit for Duplicate and Low-Value Content

Google has a limited amount of time that it spends on each website to find content. This "crawl budget" or the amount of time they will spend before moving on, can be affected by having pages that are duplicates, or just don't have value (Like archive pages, category pages, UTM parameters, tag pages, etc.). All of these types of pages should be removed from your website.

Here is how you find these types of pages:

1. Go to your preferred browser and go to Google.com.
2. Check how many pages are in Google's index by typing `site:example.com` into the Google search bar.
3. Additionally, in Google search console, check your "Indexing Coverage" report to see if there are any pages that were "crawled but not indexed" or that are labeled as "duplicates" in the report.

These "Zombie", or dead pages are best to delete or no index, doing so can improve your crawl rate and rankings.

Step 10: Check for Broken Links

A broken link is a link on your website that does not work. Broken links are basically dead ends. Have you ever gone on a website, clicked a link, and got a "404" error? Broken links are frustrating and it's important to know if you have any.

You can check for broken links by:

1. Log into your Google Search Console account.
2. Go to your "Index Coverage" report view your website's URL and identify the ones that have a 404 error.
3. Take note of the broken links and create 301 redirects.

Having too many broken links is not just troublesome for search engines, it is also a major user experience issue. This is why we often recommend to clients that when attending to technical SEO, this is one of the first things they should go about fixing.

Step 11: Check For Enhancements

When Google shows your content in the search results there may be times when they choose to show it larger, or more prominent these "rich results" can be influenced by you with structured data, or Schema markup.

To check to see if your website has structured data do this:

1. Go to Google Search console.
2. Go to the "enhancements menu", and under this menu, you can see all the structured data that is currently on your website. If there is none, then you don't have any structured data.
3. Use a schema markup generator to generate the code for the markup. For blogs use article schema, for product pages use product schema, for local businesses use local business schema. Refer to this post for more markup types to add.
4. Implement one instance of schema in the <head> HTML section of each page.

Schema markup is not only great for getting a rich snippet, but also for helping Google understand the content of your website and making your website more accessible to users.

Last Words

Now that you have a strong understanding of how to audit your website to identify key technical seo issues, next let's explore how to fix some common technical SEO issues that you may have uncovered in your auditing process.

Chapter 4: Implementation

For the next chapter let's explore common technical SEO issues and how to fix them. I used AI to identify these steps, so there are elements that mentioned in the steps that can be optimized that we didn't explore. So keep that in mind

Also, due to the rather fluid nature of SEO in general, the steps that I give to follow, may change over time, but having a basic understanding of the issues and how to fix them is a great place to start.

- **Slow Page Loading Speed**: Slow-loading pages can lead to a poor user experience and negatively impact your search rankings. Common culprits include large images, excessive JavaScript, and unoptimized code.

- **Mobile-Friendliness**: With the increasing use of mobile devices, it's crucial for your website to be mobile-friendly (responsive design). If your site doesn't display properly on mobile devices, it can harm your rankings.

- **Crawl Errors**: Issues that prevent search engine bots from crawling and indexing your site, such as broken links, redirect chains, and server errors.

- **Duplicate Content**: Having identical or very similar content on multiple pages of your website can lead to confusion for search engines and result in lower rankings.

- **URL Structure**: Poorly structured URLs can make it challenging for search engines to understand the hierarchy and organization of your site.

- **Missing or Incorrect XML Sitemaps**: A properly formatted XML sitemap helps search engines understand the structure of your website and index your pages more efficiently.

- **Robots.txt Issues**: An improperly configured robots.txt file can block search engine bots from accessing important content, preventing it from being indexed.

- **Canonicalization Errors**: Canonical tags help prevent duplicate content issues by specifying the preferred version of a page. Misuse or errors in canonical tags can lead to ranking problems.

- **SSL/HTTPS Issues**: Google gives preference to secure websites (HTTPS) over unsecured ones (HTTP). Ensure your site is properly configured with an SSL certificate.

- **Image Optimization**: Unoptimized images can slow down page loading times. Use appropriate image formats and compress images for the web.

- **Schema Markup**: Adding structured data (schema markup) to your content can enhance search results and improve click-through rates. Errors or omissions in structured data can lead to problems.

- **404 Page Not Found Errors**: Broken links that lead to 404 errors can frustrate users and negatively affect your SEO. Regularly check for and fix broken links.

- **Inconsistent Use of HTTP and WWW**: Inconsistent usage of "www" or "non-www" versions of your site can lead to duplicate content problems. You should choose one as the preferred version and use redirects.

- **Website Security**: Security issues, such as malware or hacking, can negatively impact your site's rankings and reputation.

How To Fix Slow Page Loading Speed

Fixing slow page loading speed is crucial for both user experience and SEO. Slow-loading pages can drive users away and negatively impact your search engine rankings. Here are some steps to address and improve page loading speed:

1. **Compress Images**: Large image files can significantly slow down page loading times. Use image compression tools to reduce the file size of images without sacrificing quality. Also, consider using the WebP format for images, as it is more efficient.

2. **Minimize HTTP Requests**: Each element on a web page (images, stylesheets, scripts) requires an HTTP request. Minimize these requests by combining CSS and JavaScript files, using sprites for icons, and reducing the number of images.

3. **Leverage Browser Caching**: Set up caching rules that instruct the browser to store certain files locally, so they don't need to be reloaded on subsequent visits.

4. **Enable GZIP Compression**: Enable GZIP compression on your server. This reduces the size of files sent to the browser, resulting in faster loading times.

5. **Reduce Server Response Time**: Optimize your server for faster response times. Use a content delivery network (CDN) to serve content from servers closer to the user. Ensure your hosting environment is properly configured for your website's needs.

6. **Minimize CSS and JavaScript**: Minimize and combine CSS and JavaScript files to reduce the number of requests. You can also defer non-essential scripts so they don't block the rendering of the page.

7. **Optimize Code**: Review your website's code to ensure it's clean and efficient. Remove any unnecessary code and comments. Consider using minification tools to compress HTML, CSS, and JavaScript.

8. **Use Content Delivery Networks (CDNs)**: CDNs store cached versions of your website on servers located in different geographic locations. This helps deliver content to users from a server nearest to them, reducing latency.

9. **Optimize Critical Rendering Path**: Optimize the rendering of above-the-fold content (what the user initially sees without scrolling). Prioritize loading critical resources first to improve perceived loading speed.

10. **Reduce Redirects**: Redirects add extra HTTP requests and slow down page loading. Minimize unnecessary redirects and ensure they are implemented correctly.

11. **Browser Caching**: Leverage browser caching by setting appropriate cache-control headers for your website's static resources. This helps browsers store these resources locally and retrieve them more quickly on subsequent visits.

12. **Optimize Web Fonts** Use web fonts sparingly and consider self-hosting them. Loading too many external web fonts can add to the page's loading time.

13. **Monitor Plugins and Third-Party Scripts**: Review the plugins and third-party scripts on your website. Some may be poorly optimized and slow down your site. Consider replacing or removing them if they cause performance issues.

14. **Lazy Loading**: Implement lazy loading for images and videos. This means that these resources load only when they come into the user's viewport, reducing initial loading times.

15. **Mobile Optimization**: Ensure your website is responsive and mobile-friendly. Optimize images and resources for mobile devices, as they often have slower connections.

16. **Content Delivery Optimization**: Optimize how content is delivered, such as using server push, preloading, and preconnecting to reduce latency.

17. **Regular Performance Monitoring**: Use tools like Google PageSpeed Insights, GTmetrix, or WebPageTest to regularly monitor your site's performance and address issues as they arise.

Optimizing page loading speed is an ongoing process, and it may require a combination of these techniques. Regularly testing and monitoring your site's performance is essential to ensure that your improvements are effective and that your website provides a fast and efficient user experience.

How to Improve Mobile-Friendliness

Improving mobile-friendliness is crucial in today's digital landscape since a significant portion of internet traffic comes from mobile devices. Google also prioritizes mobile-friendly websites in its search rankings. Here are some steps to improve mobile-friendliness for your website:

1. **Responsive Web Design**: Implement a responsive web design that adapts to different screen sizes and orientations. This ensures that your website looks and functions well on various mobile devices.

2. **Mobile-First Design**: Consider adopting a mobile-first design approach, where you design your website with mobile devices in mind from the start. This ensures a user-friendly experience for mobile users.

3. **Use a Mobile-Friendly CMS**: If you're using a content management system (CMS) like WordPress or Joomla,

choose a mobile-friendly theme or template. Ensure that the theme you select is responsive and optimized for mobile use.

4. **Optimize Images and Multimedia** Compress and resize images and multimedia content for faster loading on mobile devices. Use modern image formats like WebP. Implement lazy loading to ensure that images and videos load as needed to improve performance.

5. ****Mobile Navigation****: Simplify your website's navigation for mobile users. Use a mobile-friendly menu, such as a hamburger menu, to save screen space and make it easy for users to access different sections of your site.

6. **Larger Tap Targets**: Ensure that interactive elements like buttons and links have sufficiently large tap targets to make them easy to click or tap on small screens. A minimum size of 44x44 pixels is recommended.

7. **Readable Text**: Make sure text is legible on mobile screens. Use a readable font size, maintain proper line spacing, and use high-contrast text and background colors. Avoid long paragraphs.

8. **Content Prioritization**: Prioritize and present essential content and functionality at the top of the page for mobile users. This includes key information, calls to action, and contact details.

9. **Optimize Forms**: If your website uses forms, make sure they are mobile-friendly. Use input elements that are easy to select and fill out on a touch screen. Implement auto-correct and auto-suggest features for input fields.

10. **Testing and Usability:** Regularly test your website on various mobile devices and emulators to ensure it functions correctly. Pay attention to usability, and make any necessary adjustments to improve the mobile experience.

11. **Page Loading Speed**: Mobile users are often on slower connections, so optimize your site for speed. Follow the recommendations mentioned in the previous answer to improve page loading speed.

12. **Mobile SEO**: Optimize your mobile site for search engines. Ensure that your mobile pages have appropriate meta tags, structured data, and are indexed correctly.

13. **Google's Mobile-Friendly Test**: Use Google's Mobile-Friendly Test tool to assess your website's mobile-friendliness. It provides specific recommendations for improvements.

14. **Mobile Usability Reports:** Review your Google Search Console's mobile usability reports for issues that Google identifies on your site and follow their recommendations.

15. **Performance Budget**: Set performance budgets for your mobile site to ensure that it remains fast and efficient. Monitor your site's performance and make improvements when necessary.

16. **AMP (Accelerated Mobile Pages)**: Consider implementing AMP for your mobile content, especially for articles and blog posts. AMP pages are optimized for mobile speed and can lead to improved search visibility.

17. **User Testing**: Conduct usability testing with real users on mobile devices to gather feedback and make improvements based on their experience.

Improving mobile-friendliness is an ongoing process, and it's essential to keep up with best practices and adapt to changes in mobile technology and user behavior. Regular testing and user feedback can help ensure that your site provides an excellent mobile experience.

How to Fix Crawling Errors

Crawling errors can prevent search engine bots from properly indexing your website, which can negatively impact your site's visibility in search results. To fix crawling errors, follow these steps:

1. **Identify the Crawling Errors:** - Use Google Search Console (formerly Google Webmaster Tools) or other SEO tools to identify crawling errors on your website. Common errors include `404` (page not found) errors, `403` (forbidden) errors, and `500` (server) errors.

2. **404 Page Errors**: - For `404` errors, determine whether the pages were intentionally removed. If they were, consider implementing `301` redirects to direct users and search engines to relevant, equivalent pages. This can help preserve your SEO value.
- If the pages were removed unintentionally, restore them if possible, or create custom `404` error pages that guide users to other relevant content on your site.

3. **403 (Forbidden) Errors**: - Check for any issues with directory or page permissions. Make sure that the search engine bots have access to your site's content. Update your server settings if necessary.

4. **500 (Server) Errors**:- Server errors can be caused by various issues, including misconfigurations, resource limitations, or server outages. Monitor your server logs and reach out to your hosting provider or server administrator to diagnose and resolve the issue.

5. **Robot.txt File**:- Review your website's `robots.txt` file. Ensure it's not blocking important content from search

engines. Adjust it if necessary to allow access to critical pages and directories.

6. **XML Sitemaps**:- Ensure that your XML sitemaps are up to date and submitted to search engines. This helps search engine bots discover and crawl your pages more efficiently.

7. **Broken Links**: - Regularly check for broken internal and external links on your site. Fix or remove broken links to prevent crawling errors.

8. **Canonicalization Issues**:- Check for canonicalization issues. Ensure that canonical tags are correctly set to specify the preferred version of a page, reducing the likelihood of duplicate content errors.

9. **URL Structure**: - Review your URL structure and make it consistent and user-friendly. Avoid complex or dynamically generated URLs. Use descriptive, keyword-rich URLs that make sense to both users and search engines.

10. **JavaScript and AJAX Content**: - If your website relies heavily on JavaScript or AJAX for content loading, ensure that search engine bots can crawl and index this content. Provide an HTML snapshot for search engines to understand the page's content.

11. **Server Speed and Uptime**: - Ensure your web hosting is reliable, offers good server speed, and has minimal downtime. Frequent server issues can lead to crawling errors. Consider using a reliable hosting provider.

12. **Duplicate Content**:- Identify and address duplicate content issues. Use canonical tags to specify the preferred version, and ensure your content is unique and not replicated across multiple pages.

13. **Pagination**:- Properly configure pagination for content that spans multiple pages. Use `rel="next"` and `rel="prev"` tags in your pagination, and submit XML sitemaps for paginated content.

14. **Monitor and Test Regularly**: Regularly monitor your website's performance in Google Search Console and other SEO tools. Test your website using crawling and indexing tools to identify potential issues.

15. **User-Friendly Error Pages**:- Customize your error pages (`404`, `403`, etc.) to provide users with helpful information and navigation options. A well-designed error page can retain visitors and improve the user experience.

Fixing crawling errors is an ongoing process, and it's crucial to regularly monitor your website for issues and address them promptly to maintain a healthy and search-engine-friendly site.

How to Fix Duplicate Content Issues

Duplicate content issues can negatively affect your website's search engine rankings and overall user experience. Here are some steps to help you fix duplicate content issues:

1. **Identify Duplicate Content**:- Use a website crawling tool, or Google Search Console, to identify duplicate content on your website. Look for identical or substantially similar content.

2. **Canonical Tags**: - Implement canonical tags on pages with duplicate content. Canonical tags tell search engines which version of a page should be considered the original or preferred version. This helps consolidate ranking signals to the chosen page.

3. **301 Redirects**: - If you have duplicate pages that are different versions of the same content (e.g., HTTP and HTTPS or www and non-www), use 301 redirects to point one version to the other. This ensures that there's only one accessible version of the content.

4. **Use Noindex**:- For non-essential or thin content pages, consider using the "noindex" meta tag or HTTP header to prevent search engines from indexing them. This reduces the chances of duplicate content issues.

5. **Consolidate Similar Pages**:- Combine similar or overlapping pages into a single, comprehensive page. This can help reduce the occurrence of duplicate content.

8. **Avoid Duplicate Titles and Meta Descriptions**:- Ensure that each page has a unique title and meta description. This not only helps with duplicate content but also improves click-through rates in search results.

9. **Fix Syndicated or Copied Content**:- If your content is being copied or syndicated on other websites, use `rel=canonical` tags or contact the websites to request proper attribution or removal.

10. **Pagination**:- If your site uses pagination, use `rel="next"` and `rel="prev"` tags to indicate the sequence of pages, making it clear that they are part of a series. Also, set up a "view all" option if appropriate.

11. **Update XML Sitemaps**:- Ensure that your XML sitemaps only include canonical versions of your pages. This helps search engines understand your preferred content.

13. **Monitor and Maintain**:- Regularly check for new instances of duplicate content and address them promptly. Continuously monitor your site for potential issues.

By addressing duplicate content issues, you can improve your website's SEO, user experience, and overall search engine rankings. Remember that preventing duplicate content is as important as fixing existing issues.

How to Improve URL Structure

A well-structured URL can improve both user experience and search engine optimization (SEO). Here are some tips on how to improve your URL structure:

1. **Keep it Simple and Descriptive**:- Your URLs should be concise and describe the content of the page. Use clear, human-readable words that reflect the topic or purpose of the page.

2. **Use Hyphens as Separators**:- Use hyphens (-) to separate words in your URLs. Avoid underscores (_) or other characters, as hyphens are more SEO-friendly and easier for users to read.

3.**Avoid Special Characters and Spaces**:- Special characters, spaces, and symbols can cause issues with URL handling and may not be user-friendly. Stick to alphanumeric characters and hyphens.

4. **Lowercase Letters**:- URLs are case-sensitive on some servers. To avoid potential issues, use lowercase letters consistently throughout your URLs.

5. **Keyword Inclusion**:- Whenever relevant and natural, include primary keywords in your URL. This can provide a ranking signal to search engines and give users an idea of the page's content.

6. **Short and Sweet**:- Keep URLs as short as possible while still conveying the necessary information. Long, complex URLs can be confusing and less user-friendly.

7. **Consistency**:- Maintain a consistent URL structure across your website. This makes it easier for users to navigate and for search engines to understand your site's hierarchy.

8. **Avoid URL Parameters**:- Minimize the use of URL parameters (e.g., "`?id=123`") in favor of clean, static URLs. If parameters are necessary, ensure they are properly managed to avoid duplicate content issues.

9. **Subdirectories for Categorization**:- Use subdirectories to categorize content logically. For example, "`example.com/blog/`" for blog posts and "`example.com/products/`" for product pages.

10. **Canonical URLs**:- Implement canonical URLs to specify the preferred version of a page when there are multiple URL variations for the same content.

11. **No Date or Session IDs**:- Avoid including unnecessary information like publication dates or session IDs in your URLs, as this can make them less user-friendly and may not be needed for SEO.

12. **Static URLs Over Dynamic URLs**:- Whenever possible, use static URLs instead of dynamic ones. Static URLs are easier for users to understand and for search engines to index.

13. **Mobile-Friendly URLs**:- Ensure your URL structure is mobile-friendly, as more users are accessing websites via mobile devices. Short, clear URLs are even more important on small screens.

14. **301 Redirects for URL Changes**:- If you need to change a URL, implement a `301` redirect from the old URL to the new one. This ensures that both users and search engines can find the content.

15. **XML Sitemaps**:- Include your well-structured URLs in XML sitemaps to help search engines discover and index your content more efficiently.

16. **HTTPS**:- Secure your website with HTTPS. It not only provides security but also improves SEO, as search engines tend to favor secure websites.

17. **Avoid URL Parameters for Pagination**: - If you have paginated content, consider using clean URL structures with page numbers, such as "`example.com/category/page/2`," instead of query parameters.

Remember that a clear and well-structured URL can have a positive impact on both user engagement and SEO, making it easier for both users and search engines to understand and navigate your website.

How to Fix Missing or Incorrect XML Sitemaps

Fixing missing or incorrect XML sitemaps on your website is essential for search engine optimization (SEO) and ensuring search engines can crawl and index your web pages effectively. Here's a step-by-step guide to address this issue:

1. **Check Your XML Sitemap**: First, verify whether you have an XML sitemap in place. It should be located at your website's root directory (e.g., `https://www.example.com/sitemap.xml`).

2. **Generate or Update Your Sitemap**: If you don't have an XML sitemap or it's outdated, generate or update it.

3. **Validate Your Sitemap**: Before submitting your sitemap to search engines, validate it using XML sitemap validators like the one provided by Google. This ensures your sitemap follows the correct format and doesn't have errors.

4. **Submit Your Sitemap to Search Engines**: Go to each search engine console and resubmit your sitemap to ensure your site's pages are properly indexed.

5. **Check for Incorrect Sitemap Entries**: - Open your sitemap and review the URLs listed. Ensure they are accurate, and no non-indexable or duplicate pages are included.
   - Correct any incorrect URLs in your sitemap, and remove any pages that you don't want to be indexed.

6. **Robots.txt File**: Review your website's `robots.txt` file to make sure it's not blocking search engine bots from accessing your sitemap. Ensure that the sitemap's URL is allowed in the `robots.txt` file.

7. **Check for Broken Links**: Ensure that all URLs in your sitemap are functional and don't lead to 404 errors. Fix broken links and update URLs as needed.

8. **Update Your CMS and Plugins**: If you're using a content management system (CMS), ensure that your CMS and SEO plugins are up to date. Some SEO plugins generate sitemaps automatically.

9. **Check for XML Sitemap Errors**: Periodically check for XML sitemap errors in your website's code or through SEO tools. If you encounter errors, address them promptly.

10. **Regularly Monitor and Update**: XML sitemaps should be a part of your ongoing SEO efforts. Monitor your sitemap regularly, and update it when you add new content or make significant changes to your website.

By following these steps, you can fix missing or incorrect XML sitemaps and help search engines better understand your website's structure, which can lead to improved visibility and ranking in search results.

How to Fix Robots.txt Issues

Robots.txt issues can cause problems for search engine crawlers and impact the indexing of your website's content. To fix robots.txt issues, follow these steps:

1. **Identify the Issue**: - First, you need to identify the specific issue with your robots.txt file. Common issues include blocking important pages or directories, syntax errors, or accidentally disallowing search engine bots from accessing the entire site.

2. **Access Your Robots.txt File**:The robots.txt file is typically located at the root of your website. You can access it by appending "`/robots.txt`" to your domain name (e.g., `www.example.com/robots.txt`).

3. **Check for Syntax Errors**: - Open the robots.txt file using a text editor and make sure there are no syntax errors.

The file should follow the Robots Exclusion Standard (RES) syntax. It consists of "`User-agent`" and "`Disallow`" directives. Make sure each directive is properly formatted. For example:

```
User-agent: *
 Disallow: /private/
```

4. **Use Google's Robots.txt Tester**: - Google provides a Robots.txt Tester in Google Search Console that allows you to test your robots.txt file. It will highlight any issues and provide suggestions for improvement. If you're not using Google Search Console, it's a good idea to sign up and verify your site.

5. **Unblock Important Pages**: - Ensure that your robots.txt file does not block access to important pages, such as your homepage, product pages, or other high-priority content. If you find any disallow rules that shouldn't be there, remove or modify them.

6. **Allow Necessary Crawling**: - If you accidentally disallowed important directories, files, or images, adjust the "`Disallow`" directives to allow access. For example:

```
User-agent: *
 Disallow:
```

7. **Specific User-agent Rules**: - You can specify rules for specific user agents, such as Googlebot or Bingbot, if needed. Ensure that the rules for these agents are correctly configured.

8. **Test Your Changes**: - After making changes to your robots.txt file, test it using Google's Robots.txt Tester or other online tools. Ensure that it no longer has issues and that it allows search engines to access your desired content.

9. **Update the Robots.txt File**: - Once you are satisfied with your changes, update the robots.txt file on your server. Make sure it's accessible at the same URL.

10. **Monitor Your Site** :- Regularly monitor your website's performance in search engines and use tools like Google Search Console to check for any crawl errors or issues related to your robots.txt file.

Remember that while you can control which parts of your site are crawled and indexed with robots.txt, you should also use meta robots tags or other methods to provide more granular control over specific pages, if necessary. Additionally, always follow best practices for SEO and be cautious when blocking content from search engines to avoid unintended consequences.

How to Fix Canonicalization Errors

Canonicalization errors in the context of web development and SEO refer to issues where multiple URLs point to the same content, but they are not properly standardized or canonicalized. This can lead to problems with search engine rankings and user experience. Here's how to fix canonicalization errors:

1. **Choose a Preferred Domain**: - Decide whether you want your website to be accessible via the "www" subdomain or without it. For example, you can choose either "`https://example.com`" or "`https://www.example.com`" as the preferred version. Stick with one consistent choice to avoid duplication.

2. **Set Up 301 Redirects:** - Once you've chosen your preferred domain (with or without "www"), use `301` redirects to point all variations of your domain to the chosen version. This ensures that users and search engines are always directed to the same version of your site. For example, if you choose "`https://example.com`" as your preferred domain, redirect "`https://www.example.com`" to it or vice versa.

3. **Use Relative URLs**: - When creating internal links within your website, use relative URLs instead of absolute URLs. Relative URLs are shorter and ensure that links maintain consistency regardless of the domain's variations.

For example, instead of linking to "`https://www.example.com/page`," use "`/page`" as the link.

4. **Implement Canonical Tags**: - Canonical tags are HTML elements that specify the preferred version of a URL. You can add a canonical tag to the head section of your web pages to tell search engines which version of the page is the authoritative one. For example:

```html
<link rel="canonical" href="https://example.com/page">
```

This tag should point to the canonical URL of the page.

5. **Consistent URL Structure**: - Ensure that your URL structure is consistent throughout your website. Avoid using unnecessary parameters or query strings in your URLs. For example, "`https://example.com/page`" and "`https://example.com/page?source=google`" should resolve to the same content.

6. **Check for Duplicate Content**: - Regularly check for duplicate content issues on your website. Tools like Google Search Console can help you identify duplicate content errors. Address these issues by either implementing redirects or specifying canonical tags.

7. **Use Robots.txt and Sitemaps**: - Make use of the robots.txt file to instruct search engines which pages to crawl and index. Additionally, create and submit a sitemap to search engines to help them understand your website's structure and preferred URLs.

8. **Monitor and Update**: - Continuously monitor your website for canonicalization errors and fix them as they arise. Regularly update your redirects and canonical tags if necessary.

9. **Test and Validate**: - After making changes, use tools like Google Search Console,, or online SEO tools to check for canonicalization errors and validate your fixes.

By addressing canonicalization errors, you can improve your website's SEO, enhance user experience, and prevent search engines from indexing duplicate content, which can negatively impact your rankings.

How To Fix SSL/HTTPS Issues

Fixing SSL/HTTPS issues is crucial for ensuring the security and trustworthiness of your website. Here are steps to help you resolve common SSL/HTTPS issues:

1. **Identify the Problem**: - Start by identifying the specific issue you're facing. Common SSL/HTTPS problems

include expired certificates, misconfigured server settings, mixed content errors, and more.

2. **Check Certificate Validity**:
 - Ensure that your SSL certificate is valid and not expired. If it has expired, you'll need to renew it through your certificate authority (CA).

3. **Verify Certificate Chain**: - Make sure your certificate chain is complete and properly configured. This ensures that your server can verify the authenticity of your SSL certificate. It should include the SSL certificate, intermediate certificates, and the root certificate.

4. **Verify Domain Ownership**: - If you're using an extended validation (EV) or organization-validated (OV) certificate, ensure that your organization's information is up to date and correctly verified by the CA.

5. **Check Server Configuration**: - Ensure that your web server is correctly configured for SSL/HTTPS. Common web servers include Apache, Nginx, IIS, etc. The configuration may include specifying the SSL certificate file, private key, and SSL protocol settings.

6. **Update Software and Libraries**: - Keep your web server software, SSL libraries, and server operating system up to date to mitigate known vulnerabilities.

7. **Fix Mixed Content Errors**:- Mixed content occurs when your website loads both secure (HTTPS) and non-secure (HTTP) resources. This can cause security warnings. Update all links, references, and resources to use HTTPS.

8. **Check Firewall and Security Plugins**: - Sometimes, firewall or security plugins can interfere with SSL/TLS connections. Ensure that they are configured correctly and not blocking HTTPS traffic.

9. **Test Your SSL/TLS Configuration**: - Use online SSL testing tools like Qualys SSL Labs (https://www.ssllabs.com/ssltest/) to check your SSL configuration for vulnerabilities and issues. They will provide detailed reports on your SSL/TLS setup.

10. **Review Error Messages**: - Pay attention to error messages in your browser. They can often provide valuable information about the specific issue. You can use these messages to diagnose the problem.

11. **Check Server Logs**: - Examine your server logs for any error messages or warnings related to SSL/HTTPS. Server logs can often provide insights into the issue.

12. **Consult Your Hosting Provider or CA**: - If you can't resolve the issue on your own, don't hesitate to contact your web hosting provider or the certificate authority that issued

your SSL certificate. They often provide support and can help diagnose and fix the problem.

13. **Backup and Test Changes:** - Before making any changes to your server configuration, create backups, and test the changes in a safe environment. This prevents unintentional downtime or issues.

Remember that SSL/HTTPS issues can vary widely depending on your specific setup. It's important to approach the problem systematically, and if necessary, seek expert assistance to ensure your website remains secure and functional.

How to Optimize Images

Optimizing images is important for improving website performance, reducing page load times, and ensuring a good user experience. There are several techniques and best practices you can follow to optimize images:

1. **Choose the Right File Format**:- Use the appropriate image format for your content. Common formats include `JPEG`, `PNG`, and `GIF`.
   - `JPEG` is great for photographs and images with many colors.
   - `PNG` is best for images with transparency or simple graphics.

- `GIF` is for simple animations or images with a limited color palette.

2. **Resize Images**:- Use image editing software or online tools to resize images to the exact dimensions needed on your website.
   - Avoid using larger images and relying on CSS to resize them, as it can slow down page loading.

3. **Compression**:- Compress images to reduce their file size without compromising quality.

4. **Use WebP Format**:- `WebP` is a modern image format developed by Google that offers high-quality images at smaller file sizes compared to `JPEG` or `PNG`.

5. **Enable Browser Caching**: - Configure your server to use browser caching. This allows users' browsers to store images locally, reducing the need to re-download them on subsequent visits.

6. **Lazy Loading**:- Implement lazy loading for images. This defers the loading of images until they are needed (e.g., when the user scrolls down the page). Many content management systems and JavaScript libraries provide lazy loading options.

7. **Responsive Images**:- Use the `` `srcset` `` attribute in HTML to provide different image resolutions for different

device sizes and screen densities. This ensures that users receive appropriately sized images.

8. **Image Sprites**:- Combine small icons or images into a single image sprite to reduce the number of HTTP requests, which can improve loading times.

9. **Use Image CDNs**:- Content Delivery Networks (CDNs) can distribute images from servers located closer to your website's visitors, reducing latency and improving load times.

10. **Image Metadata**: - Remove unnecessary metadata from images (EXIF data). This can reduce file size.

11. **Minimize the Number of Images**:- Carefully consider whether all images are necessary on your web pages. Reducing the number of images can significantly improve load times.

12. **Test Your Website**:- Regularly test your website's performance to ensure that it is performing as intended.

Optimizing images can significantly enhance your website's performance and user experience. It's important to strike a balance between image quality and file size to ensure your website loads quickly while still looking visually appealing.

How to Fix Schema Markup Issues

Fixing schema markup issues is essential for ensuring that search engines can correctly understand and display your website's structured data in search results. Schema markup helps search engines like Google better understand the content on your website, leading to improved visibility and click-through rates. Here are the steps to fix schema markup issues:

1. **Identify the Issues**:- Start by using Google's Structured Data Testing Tool (previously known as the Structured Data Markup Helper) or other schema markup validation tools like Schema.org's Validator to identify issues on your website.
   - You can also check Google Search Console for any schema-related errors or warnings.

2. **Review Schema Markup Documentation**: - Familiarize yourself with the specific schema markup documentation relevant to your content. Schema.org provides a comprehensive list of schemas for various types of content, such as articles, products, local businesses, and more.

3. **Correct Syntax Errors**:- Inspect your schema markup for syntax errors. Ensure that your JSON-LD or microdata is properly structured and free of typos, missing brackets, or incorrect data types.

4. **Validate Data Types**: - Ensure that the data types specified in your schema markup match the content on your web page. For example, if you're marking up a recipe, make sure the ingredients and cooking times are correctly labeled as "Text," "URL," or other relevant data types.

5. **Use Structured Data Markup for Relevant Content**: - Only apply schema markup to content that's genuinely relevant to the webpage. Avoid overuse or adding markup for non-visible or irrelevant data.

6. **Ensure Data Accuracy**: - Make sure that the information provided in your schema markup matches the content on your webpage. Inaccurate or inconsistent information can lead to issues.

7. **Include All Required Properties**: - Check the schema documentation to confirm that you have included all the required properties for the specified schema type. Missing critical information can result in errors.

8. **Test and Validate**: - After making changes, revalidate your schema markup using tools like the Structured Data Testing Tool. Ensure that there are no errors or warnings.

9. **Monitor Google Search Console**: - Regularly monitor Google Search Console for any schema-related issues, errors, or warnings. Google may provide valuable insights and recommendations for improvements.

10. **Test on Multiple Devices and Browsers**: - Ensure that your schema markup is displayed correctly on different devices and browsers to accommodate various user experiences.

11. **Be Patient**: - It can take some time for search engines to recognize and process your schema markup changes. Be patient and allow time for search engines to re-crawl and re-index your content.

By following these steps and regularly maintaining your schema markup, you can help improve your website's search engine visibility and enhance the user experience.

How To Fix 404 Page Not Found Errors

Fixing a 404 Page Not Found error involves identifying the cause of the error and taking steps to resolve it. Here are some common methods to fix 404 errors on a website:

1. **Check the URL**:- The first step is to ensure that the URL you are trying to access is correct. Typos, extra spaces, or incorrect characters can lead to a 404 error. Double-check the URL for accuracy.

2. **Clear Browser Cache**: - Sometimes, a 404 error may be the result of a cached or outdated page in your web

browser. Clear your browser's cache and try accessing the page again.

3. **Verify Server Configuration**: - A `404` error can also occur if the web server is not properly configured. Check the server configuration, including the .htaccess file (if you're using Apache) or server settings (if you're using Nginx). Ensure that the server is correctly set up to handle requests.

4. **Redirects**: - If the content has been moved or renamed, make sure that there are proper redirects in place. A `301` (permanent) or `302` (temporary) redirect can be used to automatically direct users from the old URL to the new one.

5. **Check File and Directory Names**: - Make sure that the file or directory you are trying to access exists on the server and is named correctly. Case sensitivity is important in some server environments, so ensure that the capitalization of the URL matches the actual file or directory name.

6. **Broken Links**: - Review your website for broken links. Use link-checking tools or website auditing software to identify and fix broken links within your site.

7. **Content Removal or Deletion**: - If the content no longer exists, consider creating a custom `404` page to inform users that the content they were looking for is no longer

available. Include helpful links to other parts of your website.

8. **Content Restoration**: - If you accidentally deleted content or a page, consider restoring it from a backup. Regularly backing up your website can help in such situations.

9. **CMS (Content Management System) Updates**:- Ensure that your CMS and plugins are up to date. Outdated plugins or themes can lead to 404 errors.

10. **Check Server Logs**: - Examine your server logs to identify any patterns or recurring issues that could be causing 404 errors. Logs can provide valuable information about the nature of the errors.

11. **Contact Your Hosting Provider**: - If you've tried the above steps and the issue persists, contact your hosting provider for assistance. They may be able to identify server-related issues or offer guidance on fixing the problem.

12. **Monitor for External Links**: - If the 404 errors are caused by external links pointing to your website, consider setting up proper redirects or contact the websites linking to you to update their links.

13. **Custom 404 Page**: - Create a custom and user-friendly `404` error page that provides guidance to visitors. Include a search bar, site navigation links, and a message explaining that the requested page is not available.

By following these steps, you should be able to diagnose and resolve `404` Page Not Found errors on your website and improve the user experience for your visitors.

How to Fix Inconsistent Use of HTTP and WWW

Fixing inconsistent use of HTTP and WWW in URLs is important for maintaining a consistent and user-friendly web presence. Inconsistent use can confuse users and negatively impact your website's SEO. Here's how you can address this issue:

1. Choose a Preferred Format: - Decide whether you want to use URLs with "`www`" (e.g., `www.example.com`) or without "`www`" (e.g., `example.com`). This decision will become your preferred format.

2. **Configure Your Web Server**: - Depending on your web server (e.g., Apache, Nginx), configure it to enforce the use of your preferred format. This can usually be done through server configuration files. Below are steps for Apache and Nginx:

For Apache:

- Edit your .htaccess file (if using shared hosting) or the virtual host configuration file (httpd.conf or a .conf file under sites-available).
- Use mod_rewrite to enforce your preferred format. Here's an example for redirecting to "www":

```
RewriteEngine On
  RewriteCond %{HTTP_HOST} !^www\.
[NC]
  RewriteRule ^(.*)$ http://www.%
{HTTP_HOST}/$1 [R=301,L]
```

For Nginx:

- Edit your server block configuration file, usually located in `/etc/nginx/sites-available` or `/etc/nginx/conf.d`.
- Use a server block to redirect to your preferred format. For "www," you can use:

```
server {
        listen 80;
        server_name example.com;
        return 301 $scheme://
www.example.com$request_uri;
    }
    server {
        listen 80;
        server_name www.example.com;
```

```
        # Your website configuration
here
    }
```

3. **Update Internal Links**: - Review your website content, including navigation menus, and update internal links to use your preferred format consistently. This includes updating links within your HTML code, CSS files, and JavaScript.

4. **Update External Links**: - If you have control over external links (e.g., in your social media profiles or directories), update them to use your preferred format.

5. **Test Your Website**: - After making these changes, thoroughly test your website to ensure that all URLs are consistently using the format you've chosen. Check for broken links and other issues.

6. **Update SEO Settings**: - If you use SEO tools, update your settings to reflect the preferred format for your URLs. This includes updating your sitemap, robots.txt file, and settings in tools like Google Search Console.

7. **Monitor and Maintain**: - Regularly monitor your website to ensure that new content and links maintain the consistent format. Implementing `301` redirects for old

URLs and periodically checking for inconsistencies is a good practice.

By following these steps, you can ensure that your website consistently uses either "www" or the non-www format in its URLs, providing a better user experience and improving your site's SEO.

How To Fix Website Security Issues

Website security is crucial for protecting your website and the data of both you and your users. Here are some steps you can take to fix website security issues:

1. **Update Software and Plugins**: - Ensure that your website's content management system and all plugins, themes, and extensions are up to date. Outdated software can have known security vulnerabilities that attackers can exploit.

2. **Use Strong Passwords**: - Enforce strong, unique passwords for all user accounts, including administrators and users. Encourage password changes at regular intervals.

3. **Enable HTTPS**: - Install an SSL certificate to enable HTTPS on your site. This encrypts data transmitted between the user's browser and your server, enhancing data security.

4. **Implement Web Application Firewall (WAF)**: - A WAF can protect your site by filtering and monitoring incoming traffic. It helps prevent attacks such as SQL injection and cross-site scripting (XSS).

5. **Regular Backups**: - Create and maintain regular backups of your website and its databases. This will allow you to restore your site in case of a security breach or data loss.

6. **Security Plugins and Tools**: - Utilize security plugins or tools designed for your platform to scan for vulnerabilities and malware. For WordPress, you can use plugins like Wordfence or Sucuri.

7. **Disable Directory Listing**: - Ensure that directory listing is turned off. This prevents users from seeing the contents of directories on your server.

8. **SQL Injection Prevention**: - Sanitize and validate user inputs to prevent SQL injection attacks. Use prepared statements or parameterized queries to interact with your database.

9. **Cross-Site Scripting (XSS) Prevention**: - Filter and sanitize user-generated content to prevent XSS attacks. Use content security policies (CSP) to control script execution.

10. **Secure File Uploads**: - If your site allows file uploads, restrict file types, and validate them to prevent malicious uploads. Store uploaded files outside the web root.

11. **Protect Against Brute Force Attacks**: - Implement login rate limiting and CAPTCHA mechanisms to prevent brute force attacks on your login page.

12. **Security Headers**: - Configure security headers in your web server or Content Security Policy (CSP) to mitigate various attacks, including clickjacking and XSS.

13. **Remove Unused and Unnecessary Plugins and Themes**: - Unused plugins and themes can still pose security risks. Remove anything you no longer need.

14. **Monitor for Suspicious Activity**: - Set up alerts and monitoring systems to detect unusual activity on your website, such as multiple login failures.

15. **User Permissions**: - Limit user privileges and access rights to only what is necessary. Use the principle of least privilege to reduce the impact of a security breach.

16. **Error Handling**: - Customize error messages to reveal minimal information to potential attackers. Avoid exposing sensitive details in error messages.

17. **Regular Security Audits**: - Conduct regular security audits and penetration testing to identify and fix vulnerabilities.

18. **Educate Your Team**: - Train your team on security best practices to avoid common mistakes and to recognize security threats.

19. **Prepare an Incident Response Plan**: - Have a plan in place to respond to security incidents effectively. This should include steps for containing and mitigating the breach.

20. **Stay Informed**: - Keep up-to-date with security news, trends, and vulnerabilities. Subscribe to security mailing lists and follow best practices.

Remember that website security is an ongoing process. Regularly review and update your security measures to adapt to new threats and vulnerabilities. Collaborate with security professionals if necessary to ensure the highest level of protection for your website.

Last Words

Hopefully these directions can help you fix these technical issues. While these steps may be helpful there is still no possible way that following these steps will completely fix your issues. So it is important consult multiple resources to ensure that you fix your issues properly.

Closing Remarks

Congratulations on completing this Technical SEO book! This part of SEO is often the hardest to learn for beginners as it requires a high level of problem-solving and abstract thinking.

As you will soon find out as you practice technical SEO, all the components that we discussed may not be applicable *all the time*, and if they are they are only a *momentary* focus of your overall SEO strategy.

I don't say that to mitigate what you have learned, but to instead give you context that Technical SEO, is more about maintenance rather than consistent development like the other two domains of SEO are. So keep that in mind as you continue on your SEO journey.

Some additional advice I would like to give is to have a website to work on, or if you are savvy enough make one from scratch.

When I was learning, I made the decision to create a website from start to finish to practice, and it was very rewarding because it taught me about a website from a granular perspective. Which in my opinion, I believe can go miles in helping you make sense of these abstract concepts.

About the Author

Roggie (Raj) Clark, is an 8 year SEO professional and owner of the SEO agency; *Bounce Rank.* Prior to joining the SEO industry, Raj was a web developer and school teacher. It was through creating his own websites, and wanting a career change from teaching, that Raj stumbled across the world of SEO.

Since joining the field nearly a decade ago, Raj has worked on a wide range of campaigns, from eCommerce, to B2B, to Healthcare, for enterprise companies and marketing agencies in the United States.

He is regarded as an expert, and guru by his colleagues, and the SEO industry. Raj currently lives in Maryland with his sister and niece.

Consulting Or Coaching Services

I know that from reading this book, it simply may not be enough information for you or you may require more personalized support with your unique business situation.

So because of that, I'm offering the opportunity to receive consulting or coaching from me on SEO. I can offer support with:

- Creating SOPs (Standard Operating Procedures)
- Creating SEO strategies
- SEO Implementation
- Content Suggestions
- Technical Audits
- Web design/migrations
- Competitor analysis
- Keyword research
- SEO Career coaching

If you are interested in any of these services, or would like to request more information, for a specific need you may have.

Please email me at **bouncerankseo@gmail.com**. In your email, please include the following information:

- Your name
- The business you represent (if applicable)
- Team size (if applicable)
- The length of service needed
- Any other important information I should know

My administrative assistant will email you back within 24 - 48 hours with rates, and an information sheet for you to review. Thank you so much for your time and interest.

References

Adam, T. (2008, April 21). *The Art of SEO Evangelism*. Tony Adam. Retrieved December 24, 2022, from https://tonyadam.com/the-art-of-seo-evangelism/

Ahrefs. (n.d.). *What is a Noindex Tag?* Ahrefs. Retrieved December 3, 2022, from https://ahrefs.com/seo/glossary/noindex-tag

Aira. (2022). *Link Building Techniques and Tools*. Aira. Retrieved December 22, 2022, from https://aira.net/state-of-link-building/link-building-techniques-and-tools/

Avira. (n.d.). *What does error 500/503 mean? – Official Avira Support | Knowledgebase & Customer Support | Avira*. Official Avira Support. Retrieved December 5, 2022, from https://

support.avira.com/hc/en-us/articles/360000793305-What-does-error-500-503-mean-

BacklinkO. (n.d.). *Core Web Vitals: What They Are & How to Improve Them*. Backlinko. Retrieved December 4, 2022, from https://backlinko.com/hub/seo/core-web-vitals

BacklinkO. (n.d.). *Duplicate Content and SEO: The Complete Guide*. Backlinko. Retrieved December 31, 2022, from https://backlinko.com/hub/seo/duplicate-content

BacklinkO. (n.d.). *What are Backlinks? And How to Build Them in 2021*. Backlinko. Retrieved December 14, 2022, from https://backlinko.com/hub/seo/backlinks

Baggan, E. (2021, February 2). *How seasonal SERP changes affect SEO*. OnCrawl. Retrieved December

28, 2022, from https://www.oncrawl.com/technical-seo/seasonal-serp-changes-seo/

Baker, K. (2021, February 12). *What's a Subdomain & How Is It Used?* HubSpot Blog. Retrieved December 5, 2022, from https://blog.hubspot.com/website/what-is-a-subdomain

BigCommerce. (n.d.). *What are social signals? How social media impacts SEO*. BigCommerce. Retrieved December 22, 2022, from https://www.bigcommerce.com/ecommerce-answers/what-are-social-signals/

Brittanica. (n.d.). *Computer programming language - Visual Basic | Britannica*. Encyclopedia Britannica. Retrieved April 1, 2023, from https://www.britannica.com/technology/computer-programming-language/Visual-Basic#ref849838

Brockbank, J. (2012, October 29). *Losing Paradise*. Semrush. Retrieved December 5, 2022, from https://www.semrush.com/blog/subdomain-vs-subdirectory/

Bruemmer, P. (2011, December 29). *How To Get A 30% Increase In CTR With Structured Markup*. Search Engine Land. Retrieved December 5, 2022, from https://searchengineland.com/how-to-get-a-30-increase-in-ctr-with-structured-markup-105830

Caren, J. (2021, June 3). *Robots.txt: The Deceptively Important File All Websites Need*. HubSpot Blog. Retrieved December 2, 2022, from https://blog.hubspot.com/marketing/robots-txt-file

Chrome Developers. (2019, May 2). *Time to Interactive*. Chrome Developers. Retrieved December 7, 2022, from https://

developer.chrome.com/en/docs/lighthouse/performance/interactive/

Computer Hope. (2017, November 10). *What is a Domain?* Computer Hope. Retrieved December 31, 2022, from https://www.computerhope.com/jargon/d/domain.htm

Content King. (2021, October 12). *Robots.txt for SEO: Create the Best one With This 2021 Guide.* ContentKing. Retrieved April 2, 2023, from https://www.contentkingapp.com/academy/robotstxt/

Costello, R. (2020, May 7). *A/B & Multivariate Testing for SEO: How to Do It the Right Way.* Search Engine Journal. Retrieved December 28, 2022, from https://www.searchenginejournal.com/a-b-multivariate-testing-seo/366184/#close

Dean, B. (n.d.). *Search Intent and SEO: A Complete Guide*. Backlinko. Retrieved November 30, 2022, from https://backlinko.com/hub/seo/search-intent

Dean, B. (2021, October 10). *Google's 200 Ranking Factors: The Complete List (2022)*. Backlinko. Retrieved November 30, 2022, from https://backlinko.com/google-ranking-factors

Dean, B. (2022, February 26). *Link Building Case Study: How I Increased My Search Traffic by 110% in 14 Days*. Backlinko. Retrieved December 18, 2022, from https://backlinko.com/skyscraper-technique

Dean, B. (2022, October 14). *We Analyzed 4 Million Google Search Results. Here's What We Learned About Organic CTR*. Backlinko. Retrieved December 28, 2022, from https://backlinko.com/google-ctr-stats

Dennis, A. (2018, February 14). *A link-building case study: Using brand mentions and competitive linking tactics*. Search Engine Land. Retrieved December 18, 2022, from https://searchengineland.com/a-link-building-case-study-using-brand-mentions-and-competitive-linking-tactics-290048

de Valk, J. (2022, March 1). *hreflang: the ultimate guide • Yoast - Multilingual SEO*. Yoast. Retrieved December 4, 2022, from https://yoast.com/hreflang-ultimate-guide/

Doglio, F. (2020, August 12). *The JIT in JavaScript: Just In Time Compiler*. Bits and Pieces. Retrieved December 9, 2022, from https://blog.bitsrc.io/the-jit-in-javascript-just-in-time-compiler-798b66e44143

Donahole, S. (2020, November 17). *How Does My Hosting Provider Affect Site Speed*. Medium. Retrieved December 5, 2022, from https://medium.com/cornertechandmarketing/how-does-my-hosting-provider-affect-site-speed-1e05c4d98e7f

D'Ottavio, D. (2021, April 8). *Earn Press Coverage for Your Brand in 5 Steps [Case Study]*. Moz. Retrieved December 18, 2022, from https://moz.com/blog/five-steps-to-earn-press-coverage

DYNO Mapper. (n.d.). *About XML Sitemaps*. DYNO Mapper. Retrieved December 3, 2022, from https://dynomapper.com/sitemaps/amp

Eaton, B. (2022, August 19). *Web Crawlers - Top 10 Most Popular*. KeyCDN. Retrieved December 2, 2022, from https://www.keycdn.com/blog/web-crawlers

Edwards, B. (2021, August 24). *The Web Before the Web: A Look Back at Gopher*. How-To Geek. Retrieved December 7, 2022, from https://www.howtogeek.com/661871/the-web-before-the-web-a-look-back-at-gopher/

Eich, B., & Dahl, R. (n.d.). *JavaScript*. Wikipedia. Retrieved December 8, 2022, from https://en.wikipedia.org/wiki/JavaScript

Enfroy, A. (2019). *Guest Blogging in 2023: How I Wrote 80+ Guest Posts in 1 Year*. Adam Enfroy. Retrieved December 18, 2022, from https://www.adamenfroy.com/guest-blogging

Fitzgerald, A. (2020, December 28). *13 Tips for Choosing the Perfect Domain Name*. HubSpot Blog. Retrieved December 31, 2022, from https://blog.hubspot.com/website/how-to-choose-domain-name

Fultz, J. D. (2022, August 29). *What Is Average Time on Page and How to Increase It.* OptinMonster. Retrieved December 24, 2022, from https://optinmonster.com/how-to-increase-average-time-on-page/

Google Developers. (2022, September 2). *Link text | Google developer documentation style guide.* Google Developers. Retrieved December 15, 2022, from https://developers.google.com/style/link-text

Google Search Ads 360 Help. (n.d.). *GA avg time on page column - Search Ads 360 Help*. Google Support. Retrieved December 24, 2022, from https://support.google.com/searchads/answer/6125075?hl=en

Google Search Central. (n.d.). *//. //* - Wikipedia. Retrieved December 22, 2022, from https://developers.google.com/search/docs/essentials/

spam-policies?
hl=en&visit_id=638072933577621689-1687435312
&rd=1#link-spam

Google Search Central. (n.d.). *Consolidate Duplicate URLs with Canonical Tags | Google Search Central | Documentation*. Google Developers. Retrieved December 3, 2022, from https://developers.google.com/search/docs/crawling-indexing/consolidate-duplicate-urls

Google Search Central. (n.d.). *Core Web Vitals report - Search Console Help*. Google Support. Retrieved December 4, 2022, from https://support.google.com/webmasters/answer/9205520?hl=en

Google Search Central. (n.d.). *Core Web Vitals report - Search Console Help*. Google Support. Retrieved December 4, 2022, from https://

support.google.com/webmasters/answer/9205520?hl=en

Google Search Central. (n.d.). *Crawl Budget Management For Large Sites | Google Search Central | Documentation.* Google Developers. Retrieved December 28, 2022, from https://developers.google.com/search/docs/crawling-indexing/large-site-managing-crawl-budget

Google Search Central. (n.d.). *Google URL Structure Guidelines | Google Search Central | Documentation.* Google Developers. Retrieved March 19, 2023, from https://developers.google.com/search/docs/crawling-indexing/url-structure

Google Search Central. (n.d.). *Headings and titles | Google developer documentation style guide.*

Google Developers. Retrieved April 4, 2023, from https://developers.google.com/style/headings

Google Search Central. (n.d.). *How to Write Meta Descriptions | Google Search Central | Documentation*. Google Developers. Retrieved December 14, 2022, from https://developers.google.com/search/docs/appearance/snippet

Google Search Central. (n.d.). *How to Write Meta Descriptions | Google Search Central | Documentation*. Google Developers. Retrieved December 15, 2022, from https://developers.google.com/search/docs/appearance/snippet

Google Search Central. (n.d.). *In-Depth Guide to How Google Search Works | Google Search Central | Documentation*. Google Developers. Retrieved

December 12, 2022, from https://developers.google.com/search/docs/fundamentals/how-search-works

Google Search Central. (n.d.). *Influencing Title Links in Google Search | Google Search Central | Documentation*. Google Developers. Retrieved December 15, 2022, from https://developers.google.com/search/docs/appearance/title-link

Google Search Central. (n.d.). *Learn About What Sitelinks Are | Google Search Central | Documentation*. Google Developers. Retrieved December 14, 2022, from https://developers.google.com/search/docs/appearance/sitelinks

Google Search Central. (n.d.). *What Is a Sitemap | Google Search Central | Documentation*. Google

Developers. Retrieved December 3, 2022, from https://developers.google.com/search/docs/crawling-indexing/sitemaps/overview

Google Search Central. (2017, December 21). *Subdomain or subfolder, which is better for SEO?* YouTube. Retrieved December 5, 2022, from https://www.youtube.com/watch?v=uJGDyAN9g-g&feature=emb_title

Google Search Central. (2020, July 11). *English Google Webmaster Central office-hours from September 27, 2019*. YouTube. Retrieved December 14, 2022, from https://www.youtube.com/watch?v=rwpwq8Ynf7s&t=1427s

Google Search Central. (2022, August 23). *Structured data for web developers | Search Central Lightning Talks*. YouTube. Retrieved Decemeber 5,

2022, from https://www.youtube.com/watch?v=hUHjeDylhE8&t=65s

Google Search Central. (2022, 11). *Robots.txt Introduction and Guide | Google Search Central | Documentation*. Google Developers. Retrieved December 2, 2022, from https://developers.google.com/search/docs/crawling-indexing/robots/intro

Google Search Central. (2023, 2). *Block Search Indexing with noindex | Google Search Central | Documentation*. Google Developers. Retrieved March 24, 2023, from https://developers.google.com/search/docs/crawling-indexing/block-indexing

Google Search CentralSe. (n.d.). *Google Image SEO Best Practices | Google Search Central | Documentation*. Google Developers. Retrieved

December 15, 2022, from https://developers.google.com/search/docs/appearance/google-images

Google Search Console Help. (n.d.). *Manual Actions report - Search Console Help*. Google Support. Retrieved December 23, 2022, from https://support.google.com/webmasters/answer/9044175?hl=en#zippy=%2Cunnatural-links-to-your-site

Google Search Console Help. (n.d.). *What are impressions, position, and clicks? - Search Console Help*. Google Support. Retrieved December 24, 2022, from https://support.google.com/webmasters/answer/7042828?hl=en#impressions

Google Support. (n.d.). *Indexing - Search Console Help*. Google Support. Retrieved December 2,

2022, from https://support.google.com/webmasters/answer/7645831?hl=en

Gorham, J. (2020, August 12). *HARO Link Building Case Study: How I Built 33 Links In 6 Hours*. Engine Scout. Retrieved December 18, 2022, from https://enginescout.com.au/10-minute-backlinks/

Gotch, N. (2022, October 2). *How to Start an SEO Business in 2022 (A-Z Process)*. Gotch SEO. Retrieved December 30, 2022, from https://www.gotchseo.com/start-seo-company/

Hall, M. (2022, November 3). *Google | History & Facts | Britannica*. Encyclopedia Britannica. Retrieved December 7, 2022, from https://www.britannica.com/topic/Google-Inc

Hardwick, J. (2022, May 23). *Broken Link Building: The Complete Guide*. Ahrefs. Retrieved December

22, 2022, from https://ahrefs.com/blog/broken-link-building/

Hardwick, J., & Mueller, J. (2020, April 14). *Canonical Tags: A Simple Guide for Beginners.* Ahrefs. Retrieved December 28, 2022, from https://ahrefs.com/blog/canonical-tags/

Harvard University. (n.d.). *Write good Alt Text to describe images.* Harvard's Digital Accessibility Services. Retrieved December 14, 2022, from https://accessibility.huit.harvard.edu/describe-content-images

Haverbeke, M. (2018). *Values, Types, and Operators*. Eloquent JavaScript. Retrieved March 27, 2023, from https://eloquentjavascript.net/01_values.html

Headings and titles | Google developer documentation style guide. (2022, August 5).

Google Developers. Retrieved December 14, 2022, from https://developers.google.com/style/headings

Hendriks, M. (2022, August 11). *What is an XML sitemap and why should you have one?* Yoast. Retrieved December 3, 2022, from https://yoast.com/what-is-an-xml-sitemap-and-why-should-you-have-one/

Hlopov, N. (2021, May 19). *How to include CSS to a page (with Pros and Cons)*. Nikita Hlopov. Retrieved December 9, 2022, from https://nikitahl.com/how-to-include-css-to-a-page

Hoffmann, J. (2017, October 22). *A Look Back at the History of CSS | CSS-Tricks*. CSS-Tricks. Retrieved December 8, 2022, from https://css-tricks.com/look-back-history-css/

Holmes, T. (2022, December 1). *What is a Subdirectory? (with pictures)*. EasyTechJunkie.

Retrieved December 5, 2022, from https://www.easytechjunkie.com/what-is-a-subdirectory.htm

IBM. (n.d.). *Home*. YouTube. Retrieved December 9, 2022, from https://www.ibm.com/docs/en/zos/2.1.0?topic=program-string-values

Indig, K. (2022, February 7). *What Is Technical SEO? Your Guide to Getting Started*. SEMrush. Retrieved November 30, 2022, from https://www.semrush.com/blog/learning-technical-seo/

JavaScript Basics (2022 Tutorial & Examples). (n.d.). BrainStation. Retrieved December 9, 2022, from https://brainstation.io/learn/javascript/basics

K, V. (2021, October 1). *JavaScript : Advantages and disadvantages of External JavaScript ?* scmGalaxy. Retrieved December 9, 2022, from https://www.scmgalaxy.com/tutorials/javascript-advantages-and-disadvantages-of-external-javascript/

Kim, L. (2022, November 12). *What Is a Good Conversion Rate? It's Higher Than You Think!* WordStream. Retrieved December 27, 2022, from https://www.wordstream.com/blog/ws/2014/03/17/what-is-a-good-conversion-rate

Krishnan, J., & Chang, W.-T. (2021, June 7). *Using AVIF to compress images on your site*. web.dev. Retrieved December 12, 2022, from https://web.dev/compress-images-avif/

Lahey, C. (2021, March 30). *History of the Most Important Google Algorithm Updates*. Semrush. Retrieved December 7, 2022, from https://www.semrush.com/blog/google-algorithm-update/

Larkin, K. (2022, June 29). *What Is The Difference Between Search Queries And Keywords?* Search

Engine Journal. Retrieved March 18, 2023, from https://www.searchenginejournal.com/understanding-difference-queries-keywords/126421/#close

Leist, R. (2022, January 7). *How to Do Keyword Research for SEO: A Beginner's Guide*. HubSpot Blog. Retrieved November 30, 2022, from https://blog.hubspot.com/marketing/how-to-do-keyword-research-ht

Lyons, K. (2022, July 6). *Long-Tail Keywords: What They Are & How to Use Them for SEO.* SEMrush. Retrieved November 30, 2022, from https://www.semrush.com/blog/how-to-choose-long-tail-keywords/

Marchant, R. (2016, June 3). *Citation building the most popular link building tactic for Local SEOs*. BrightLocal. Retrieved December 18, 2022, from https://www.brightlocal.com/research/citation-building-rated-the-most-popular-link-building-tactic-for-local-seos/

MDN contributors. (2022, September 20). *First contentful paint - MDN Web Docs Glossary: Definitions of Web-related terms | MDN*. MDN Web Docs. Retrieved December 7, 2022, from https://developer.mozilla.org/en-US/docs/Glossary/First_contentful_paint

Melnick, M. (2017, September 29). *Web 101: Common HTML Elements*. Wingard. Retrieved December 8, 2022, from https://wearewingard.com/web-101-common-html-elements/

Merriam webster. (n.d.). *Competency Definition & Meaning*. Merriam-Webster. Retrieved December 29, 2022, from https://www.merriam-webster.com/dictionary/competency

Meyers, P. J. (2019, May 14). *How Often Does Google Update Its Algorithm?* Moz. Retrieved November 30, 2022, from https://moz.com/blog/how-often-does-google-update-its-algorithm

Meyers, P. J. (2019, May 14). *How Often Does Google Update Its Algorithm?* Moz. Retrieved December 28, 2022, from https://moz.com/blog/how-often-does-google-update-its-algorithm

Monaghan, M. (2022, October 27). *Website Load Time Statistics: Why Speed Matters in 2022.* Website Builder Expert. Retrieved November 30, 2022, from https://www.websitebuilderexpert.com/building-websites/website-load-time-statistics/

Moriarty, B. (2022, April 15). *Storytelling in Business: How to Create Engaging Stories | Darden Ideas to Action.* Darden Ideas to Action. Retrieved December 28, 2022, from https://

ideas.darden.virginia.edu/storytelling-in-business-engaging-stories

Moz. (n.d.). *Domain Authority: What is it and how is it calculated.* Moz. Retrieved December 27, 2022, from https://moz.com/learn/seo/domain-authority

Moz. (n.d.). *Internal Links SEO Best Practices.* Moz. Retrieved December 14, 2022, from https://moz.com/learn/seo/internal-link

Moz. (n.d.). *What Are External Links? Best Practices For Building Authority.* Moz. Retrieved December 14, 2022, from https://moz.com/learn/seo/external-link

Moz. (n.d.). *What Are Keywords And Why Are They Important For SEO?* Moz. Retrieved November 30, 2022, from https://moz.com/learn/seo/what-are-keywords

Moz. (n.d.). *What Is A URL And Why Do They Matter For SEO?* Moz. Retrieved December 3, 2022, from https://moz.com/learn/seo/url

Moz. (n.d.). *What Is Conversion Rate Optimization? How To Calculate CRO*. Moz. Retrieved December 27, 2022, from https://moz.com/learn/seo/conversion-rate-optimization

Moz. (n.d.). *What Is On-Site SEO? How To Optimize A Page*. Moz. Retrieved December 12, 2022, from https://moz.com/learn/seo/on-site-seo

Mozilla. (2022, September 14). *What is JavaScript? - Learn web development | MDN*. MDN Web Docs. Retrieved December 8, 2022, from https://developer.mozilla.org/en-US/docs/Learn/JavaScript/First_steps/What_is_JavaScript

Mozilla Developer. (2022, August 29). *Link types: noopener - HTML: HyperText Markup Language |*

MDN. MDN Web Docs. Retrieved December 22, 2022, from https://developer.mozilla.org/en-US/docs/Web/HTML/Link_types/noopener

Mozilla Developer. (2022, October 30). *Functions - JavaScript | MDN*. MDN Web Docs. Retrieved December 9, 2022, from https://developer.mozilla.org/en-US/docs/Web/JavaScript/Guide/Functions

Mueller, J. (2021, August 23). *🦇 johnmu: cats are not people 🦇 on Twitter: "@The_Scorpionboy No effect on SEO. Like ads, like social media. It's good to have multiple separate sources of traffic to your website, and not everything needs to have an SEO effect."* Twitter. Retrieved December 22, 2022, from https://twitter.com/JohnMu/status/1429847035319103493

Nelson, C. (n.d.). *What creators should know about Google's August 2022 helpful content update | Google Search Central Blog*. Google Developers. Retrieved December 7, 2022, from https://developers.google.com/search/blog/2022/08/helpful-content-update

Oh, S. (2021, July 14). *Case Study: Does Broken Link Building Work Today?* YouTube. Retrieved December 22, 2022, from https://www.youtube.com/watch?v=k_0jmRvK4gs

Osmani, A., & Pollard, B. (2022, October 25). *Optimize Cumulative Layout Shift*. web.dev. Retrieved December 5, 2022, from https://web.dev/optimize-cls/

Patel, N. (n.d.). *How to Boost Your SEO by Using Schema Markup*. Neil Patel. Retrieved December 5,

2022, from https://neilpatel.com/blog/get-started-using-schema/

Patrick, S. (n.d.). *Importance of Geotagging your Keywords for SEO*. SEO Hacker. Retrieved November 30, 2022, from https://seo-hacker.com/keyword-geotagging-seo/

Payne, J. (2021, August 26). *What is a 301 Redirect, and When Should You Use One?* HubSpot Blog. Retrieved December 5, 2022, from https://blog.hubspot.com/blog/tabid/6307/bid/7430/what-is-a-301-redirect-and-why-should-you-care.aspx

Pernice, K. (2017, November 12). *F-Shaped Pattern of Reading on the Web: Misunderstood, But Still Relevant (Even on Mobile)*. Nielsen Norman Group. Retrieved December 17, 2022, from https://www.nngroup.com/articles/f-shaped-pattern-reading-web-content/

PluralSight. (n.d.). *JavaScript Conditionals: The Basics with Examples*. JavaScript.com. Retrieved December 9, 2022, from https://www.javascript.com/learn/conditionals

Pokorny, E. (2022, March 11). *Hreflang language codes: 2022 list and how to use them*. Weglot Translate. Retrieved December 4, 2022, from https://weglot.com/blog/hreflang-language-codes-2022-list-and-how-to-use-them/

Rankin, T. (2019, June 27). How to Optimize JavaScript and CSS and Improve Website Performance. Retrieved December 9, 2022, from https://torquemag.io/2019/06/optimize-javascript-css/

Rocket Content. (2020, September 30). *Largest Contentful Paint (LCP): what it is and how to improve it*. Rock Content. Retrieved December 5,

2022, from https://rockcontent.com/blog/largest-contentful-paint/

Search engine. (n.d.). Wikipedia. Retrieved November 30, 2022, from https://en.wikipedia.org/wiki/Search_engine

Searchmetrics. (n.d.). *Conversion – SEO Glossary*. Searchmetrics. Retrieved December 27, 2022, from https://www.searchmetrics.com/glossary/conversion/

Search Metrics. (2022). *Search volume - find the definition in the SEO Glossary*. Searchmetrics. Retrieved November 30, 2022, from https://www.searchmetrics.com/glossary/search-volume/

Seer interactive. (2022, March 14). *How to Use SEMRush to Identify Search Trends and Competitor Insights*. Seer Interactive. Retrieved December 28, 2022, from https://www.seerinteractive.com/

insights/how-to-use-semrush-to-identify-search-trends-and-competitor-insights

SEO Keywords. (n.d.). WooRank. Retrieved November 30, 2022, from https://www.woorank.com/en/edu/seo-guides/what-are-keywords-in-seo

Sickler, J. (2021, April 30). *What is E-A-T & Why it's Important (Google, E-A-T and SEO)*. Terakeet. Retrieved November 30, 2022, from https://terakeet.com/blog/what-is-eat/

Silva, C. (2022, December 12). What Is Off-Page SEO? A Guide to Off-Page SEO Strategy. Semrush. Retrieved April 8, 2023, from https://www.semrush.com/blog/off-page-seo/

Slawski, B., Slawski's, B., & slawski, b. (2006, February 5). *What was the First Search Engine?* SEO by the Sea. Retrieved December 7, 2022, from https://www.seobythesea.com/2006/02/just-what-was-the-first-search-engine/

Soulo, T. (2022, May 9). *Keyword Difficulty: How to Estimate Your Chances to Rank.* Ahrefs. Retrieved November 30, 2022, from https://ahrefs.com/blog/keyword-difficulty/

Soulo, T. (2022, September 13). *Keyword Research: The Beginner's Guide by Ahrefs*. Ahrefs. Retrieved November 30, 2022, from https://ahrefs.com/blog/keyword-research/

Southern, M. G. (2020, September 15). *Google's John Mueller: Keywords in Domain Name Aren't Needed.* Search Engine Journal. Retrieved December 31, 2022, from https://www.searchenginejournal.com/keywords-in-domain-name/380912/#close

Southern, M. G. (2022, December 15). *Google E-E-A-T: How To Demonstrate First-Hand Experience*. Search Engine Journal. Retrieved January 15, 2023, from https://www.searchenginejournal.com/google-e-e-a-t-how-to-demonstrate-first-hand-experience/474446/

Spinutech. (2018, June 14). *SEO FAQ: Keyword Rankings Explained*. Spinutech. Retrieved December 27, 2022, from https://www.spinutech.com/digital-marketing/seo/analytics/seo-faq-keyword-rankings-explained/

Stanford, L. (n.d.). *US6285999B1 - Method for node ranking in a linked database*. Google Patents. Retrieved December 17, 2022, from https://patents.google.com/patent/US6285999

Stox, P. (2022, February 23). *What Are Core Web Vitals & How Can You Improve Them?* Ahrefs.

Retrieved December 4, 2022, from https://ahrefs.com/blog/core-web-vitals/

Sullivan, D. (n.d.). *Evolving "nofollow" – new ways to identify the nature of links | Google Search Central Blog*. Google Developers. Retrieved December 22, 2022, from https://developers.google.com/search/blog/2019/09/evolving-nofollow-new-ways-to-identify

Sullivan, D. (2019, August 01). *What site owners should know about Google's August 2019 core update | Google Search Central Blog*. Google Developers. Retrieved November 30, 2022, from https://developers.google.com/search/blog/2019/08/core-updates

Sullivan, D. (2022, May 25). *May 2022 core update releasing for Google Search | Google Search Central Blog*. Google Developers. Retrieved

November 30, 2022, from https://developers.google.com/search/blog/2022/05/may-2022-core-update

Sullivan, D. (2022, August 18). *More content by people, for people in Search*. The Keyword. Retrieved November 30, 2022, from https://blog.google/products/search/more-content-by-people-for-people-in-search/

Theuring, J. (2022, October 12). *Bing vs Google: Search Engine Comparison 2022*. Impression. Retrieved December 7, 2022, from https://www.impression.co.uk/blog/bing-differ-google/

Tutorial Republic. (n.d.). *Adding JavaScript to HTML Document*. Tutorial Republic. Retrieved December 9, 2022, from https://www.tutorialrepublic.com/javascript-tutorial/javascript-get-started.php

Tutorialspoint. (n.d.). *JavaScript - Syntax*. Tutorialspoint. Retrieved December 8, 2022, from https://www.tutorialspoint.com/javascript/javascript_syntax.htm

Tutorials Teacher. (n.d.). *JavaScript Variables (With Examples)*. TutorialsTeacher. Retrieved December 9, 2022, from https://www.tutorialsteacher.com/javascript/javascript-variable

Ugor, M. (2022, June 7). *600000 Link Outreach Emails Analyzed: Here"s What Works*. Authority Hacker. Retrieved December 18, 2022, from https://www.authorityhacker.com/link-building-outreach/

Vura, T. (n.d.). *Google Algorithm Updates: A Running Timeline of Major Changes*. BrightEdge. Retrieved November 30, 2022, from https://www.brightedge.com/blog/google-algorithm-updates-running-timeline-major-changes

W3school. (n.d.). *HTML Styles CSS*. W3Schools. Retrieved December 9, 2022, from https://www.w3schools.com/html/html_css.asp

W3School. (n.d.). *HTML Tutorial*. W3Schools. Retrieved December 9, 2022, from https://www.w3schools.com/html/default.asp

W3School. (n.d.). *JavaScript Events*. W3Schools. Retrieved December 9, 2022, from https://www.w3schools.com/js/js_events.asp

W3School. (n.d.). *JavaScript Statements*. W3Schools. Retrieved December 9, 2022, from https://www.w3schools.com/js/js_statements.asp

W3school. (n.d.). *What is JavaScript*. W3Schools. Retrieved December 8, 2022, from https://www.w3schools.com/whatis/whatis_js.asp

W3Schools. (n.d.). *JavaScript Functions*. W3Schools. Retrieved March 29, 2023, from https://www.w3schools.com/js/js_functions.asp

Walden, H. (2022, April 14). *What Does the rel="noopener noreferrer" Tag Mean? (& Does It Affect SEO?)*. Elegant Themes. Retrieved December 22, 2022, from https://www.elegantthemes.com/blog/wordpress/rel-noopener-noreferrer-nofollow

Wall, A. (2017). *Search Engine History*. Search Engine History.com. Retrieved December 7, 2022, from http://www.searchenginehistory.com/#search-work

Walton, P. (2019, June 11). *Cumulative Layout Shift (CLS)*. web.dev. Retrieved December 5, 2022, from https://web.dev/cls/

Walton, P. (2019, November 7). *First Input Delay (FID)*. web.dev. Retrieved December 5, 2022, from https://web.dev/fid/

Walton, P., & Pollard, B. (2022, September 27). *Optimize Largest Contentful Paint*. web.dev. Retrieved December 5, 2022, from https://web.dev/optimize-lcp/

Webfx. (n.d.). *Why Search Intent Matters for SEO (Plus 3 Optimization Tips)*. WebFX. Retrieved November 30, 2022, from https://www.webfx.com/seo/learn/why-search-intent-matters-to-seo/

What Are Title Tags? [Plus FREE Title Tag Preview Tool]. (n.d.). Moz. Retrieved December 13, 2022, from https://moz.com/learn/seo/title-tag

Wikipedia. (n.d.). *Anchor text*. Wikipedia. Retrieved December 14, 2022, from https://en.wikipedia.org/wiki/Anchor_text

Wikipedia. (n.d.). *CSS*. Wikipedia. Retrieved December 8, 2022, from https://en.wikipedia.org/wiki/CSS

Wikipedia. (n.d.). *Domain authority*. Wikipedia. Retrieved December 27, 2022, from https://en.wikipedia.org/wiki/Domain_authority

Wikipedia. (n.d.). *HTML*. Wikipedia. Retrieved December 8, 2022, from https://en.wikipedia.org/wiki/HTML

Wikipedia. (n.d.). *JumpStation*. Wikipedia. Retrieved December 7, 2022, from https://en.wikipedia.org/wiki/JumpStation

Wikipedia. (n.d.). *MSN*. Wikipedia. Retrieved December 7, 2022, from https://en.wikipedia.org/wiki/MSN

Wikipedia. (n.d.). *Performance indicator*. Wikipedia. Retrieved December 24, 2022, from https://en.wikipedia.org/wiki/Performance_indicator

Wikipedia. (n.d.). *URL*. Wikipedia. Retrieved December 3, 2022, from https://en.wikipedia.org/wiki/URL

Wikipedia. (n.d.). *Web hosting service*. Wikipedia. Retrieved December 5, 2022, from https://en.wikipedia.org/wiki/Web_hosting_service

Wikipedia. (n.d.). *World Wide Web*. Wikipedia. Retrieved December 3, 2022, from https://en.wikipedia.org/wiki/World_Wide_Web

Wikipedia. (n.d.). *World Wide Web*. Wikipedia. Retrieved December 7, 2022, from https://en.wikipedia.org/wiki/World_Wide_Web

Wikipedia. (n.d.). *World Wide Web Worm*. Wikipedia. Retrieved December 7, 2022, from https://en.wikipedia.org/wiki/World_Wide_Web_Worm

Wikipedia. (n.d.). *Yahoo! Search*. Wikipedia. Retrieved December 7, 2022, from https://en.wikipedia.org/wiki/Yahoo!_Search

Woorank. (n.d.). *What is an XML Sitemap?* WooRank. Retrieved December 3, 2022, from https://www.woorank.com/en/edu/seo-guides/xml-sitemaps

Xu, L. (2018, January 10). *9 Most Common Schema Markup Types*. Overdrive Interactive. Retrieved December 5, 2022, from https://www.ovrdrv.com/blog/9-most-common-schema-markup-types/

Yoast. (2021, September 22). *Long-tail keywords: why they deserve your focus! • Yoast*. Yoast. Retrieved November 30, 2022, from https://yoast.com/focus-on-long-tail-keywords/

www.ingramcontent.com/pod-product-compliance
Lightning Source LLC
LaVergne TN
LVHW022049200926
848481LV00003B/839